92
Fra

Amdur, Richard
  Anne Frank.   Chelsea House [c1993]
111p illus (Chelsea House lib of
biography)

Traces the life of the young Jewish
girl whose diary chronicles the years
she and her family hid from the Nazis
in an Amsterdam attic.   Bibliog

1 Frank, Anne   2 Holocaust, Jewish
(1933-1945)--Biography 3 Jews--
Amsterdam (Netherlands)--Biography
4 Amsterdam (Netherlands)--Biography
I T

ISBN 0-7910-1641-2   lib. bdg.
                                         LCCN 92-5028
009587 26-819-05   817242   ME © BAKER & TAYLOR Books   3191

ANNE FRANK

THE CHELSEA HOUSE LIBRARY OF BIOGRAPHY

ANNE FRANK

RICHARD AMDUR

Chelsea House Publishers

New York • Philadelphia

CHELSEA HOUSE PUBLISHERS

Editor-in-Chief   Richard S. Papale
Managing Editor   Karyn Gullen Browne
Copy Chief   Philip Koslow
Picture Editor   Adrian Allen
Art Director   Maria Epes
Assistant Art Director   Howard Brotman
Manufacturing Director   Gerald Levine
Systems Manager   Lindsey Ottman
Production Coordinator   Marie Claire Cebrián-Ume

The Chelsea House Library of Biography
Senior Editor   Kathy Kuhtz

Staff for ANNE FRANK
Copy Editor   Christopher Duffy
Editorial Assistant   Nicole A. Garfield
Picture Researcher   Ellen Barrett
Series Designer   Basia Niemczyc
Cover Illustration   Daniel Mark Duffy

Printed and bound in Mexico.

First Printing

1   3   5   7   9   8   6   4   2

Library of Congress Cataloging-in-Publication Data

Amdur, Richard
Anne Frank/by Richard Amdur: with an introduction by Vito Perrone.
p. cm.—(The Chelsea House library of biography)
Includes bibliographical references and index.
Traces the life of the young Jewish girl whose diary chronicles the years she and
her family hid from the Nazis in an Amsterdam attic.
ISBN 0-7910-1641-2
       0-7910-1645-5 (pbk.)
1. Frank, Anne, 1929–1945—Juvenile literature. 2. Holocaust, Jewish, 1939–
1945—Netherlands—Amsterdam—Biography—Juvenile literature. 3. Jews—
Netherlands—Amsterdam—Biography—Juvenile Literature. 4. Amsterdam
(Netherlands)—Biography—Juvenile Literature. [1. Frank, Anne, 1929–1945.
2. Jews—Biography. 3. Holocaust, Jewish, 1939–1945—Netherlands—
Amsterdam.] I. Title. II. Series.
DS135.N6F7315 1992   92-5028
940.53'18'092—dc20   CIP
[B]   AC

Contents

THE CHELSEA HOUSE LIBRARY OF BIOGRAPHY

Other titles in the series are forthcoming.

Introduction

Learning from Biographies

Vito Perrone

The oldest narratives that exist are biographical. Much of what we know, for example, about the Pharaohs of ancient Egypt, the builders of Babylon, the philosophers of Greece, the rulers of Rome, the many biblical and religious leaders who provide the base for contemporary spiritual beliefs, has come to us through biographies—the stories of their lives. Although an oral tradition was long the mainstay of historically important biographical accounts, the oral stories making up this tradition became by the 1st century A.D. central elements of a growing written literature.

In the 1st century A.D., biography assumed a more formal quality through the work of such writers as Plutarch, who left us more than 500 biographies of political and intellectual leaders of Rome and Greece. This tradition of focusing on great personages lasted well into the 20th century and is seen as an important means of understanding the history of various times and places. We learn much, for example, from Plutarch's writing about the collapse of the Greek city-states and about the struggles in Rome over the justice and the constitutionality of a world empire. We also gain considerable understanding of the definitions of morality and civic virtue and how various common men and women lived out their daily existence.

Not surprisingly, the earliest American writing, beginning in the 17th century, was heavily biographical. Those Europeans who came to America were dedicated to recording their experience, especially the struggles they faced in building what they determined to be a new culture. John Norton's *Life and Death of John Cotton*, printed in 1630, typifies these early works. Later biographers often tackled more ambitious projects. Cotton Mather's *Magnalia Christi Americana*, published in 1702, accounted for the lives of more than 70 ministers and political leaders. In addition, a biographical literature around the theme of Indian captivity had considerable popularity. Soon after the American Revolution and the organization of the United States of America, Americans were treated to a large outpouring of biographies about such figures as Benjamin Franklin, George Washington, Thomas Jefferson, and Aaron Burr, among others. These particular works served to build a strong sense of national identity.

Among the diverse forms of historical literature, biographies have been over many centuries the most popular. And in recent years interest in biography has grown even greater, as biography has gone beyond prominent government figures, military leaders, giants of business, industry, literature, and the arts. Today we are treated increasingly to biographies of more common people who have inspired others by their particular acts of courage, by their positions on important social and political issues, or by their dedicated lives as teachers, town physicians, mothers, and fathers. Through this broader biographical literature, much of which is featured in the CHELSEA HOUSE LIBRARY OF BIOGRAPHY, our historical understandings can be enriched greatly.

What makes biography so compelling? Most important, biography is a human story. In this regard, it makes of history something personal, a narrative with which we can make an intimate connection. Biographers typically ask us as readers to accompany them on a journey through the life of another person, to see some part of the world through another's eyes. We can, as a result, come to understand what it is like to live the life of a slave, a farmer, a textile worker, an engineer, a poet, a president—in a sense, to walk in another's shoes. Such experience can be personally invaluable. We cannot ask for a better entry into historical studies.

Although our personal lives are likely not as full as those we are reading about, there will be in most biographical accounts many common experiences. As with the principal character of any biography, we are also faced with numerous decisions, large and small. In the midst of living our lives we are not usually able to comprehend easily the significance of our daily decisions or grasp easily their many possible consequences, but we can gain important insights into them by seeing the decisions made by others play themselves out. We can learn from others.

Because biography is a personal story, it is almost always full of surprises. So often, the personal lives of individuals we come across historically are out of view, their public personas masking who they are. It is through biography that we gain access to their private lives, to the acts that define who they are and what they truly care about. We see their struggles within the possibilities and limitations of life, gaining insight into their beliefs, the ways they survived hardships, what motivated them, and what discouraged them. In the process we can come to understand better our own struggles.

As you read this biography, try to place yourself within the subject's world. See the events as that person sees them. Try to understand why the individual made particular decisions and not others. Ask yourself if you would have chosen differently. What are the values or beliefs that guide the subject's actions? How are those values or beliefs similar to yours? How are they different from yours? Above all, remember: You are engaging in an important historical inquiry as you read a biography, but you are also reading a literature that raises important personal questions for you to consider.

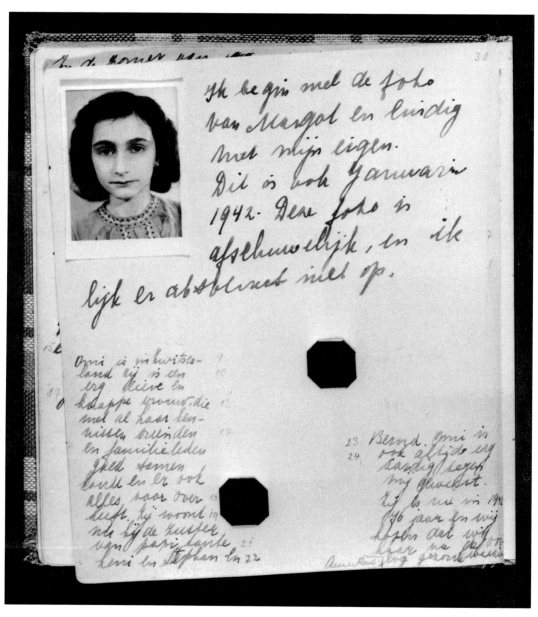

A page from Anne Frank's diary shows a snapshot of her. Anne received the diary as a present on her 13th birthday. She kept a detailed record of her life in hiding, including observations about her family and about events in the German-occupied Netherlands.

1

Fear Visits a Family in Hiding

"LIGHTS OUT . . . WE EXPECT THE POLICE in the house!" Anne Frank heard her father's instructions and the panic in his voice. But Otto Frank had vanished as quickly as he had first appeared, leaving Anne without an explanation. She wondered what was happening. Were there burglars on the premises? Had someone discovered their hiding place? Was the family's great secret about to be exposed?

The lights were put out, and Anne, 14 years old, huddled with her mother, her 18-year-old sister, Margot, and Mrs. Van Daan, a family friend. The frightened women whispered nervously about the awful possibilities. As the minutes passed they quieted down. Then they heard a bang. The color drained from their faces as they waited for the four men—Otto Frank, Hermann Van Daan, the Van Daans' son, Peter, and Albert Dussell, another friend of the Franks'—to return. Anne had never been so scared in her life.

It was 10 o'clock in the evening of April 9, 1944—
Easter Sunday. With the exception of the four people who
were helping them hide, no one had seen the eight Dutch
Jews for many, many months. That is how long Anne and
the others had succeeded in hiding from the Nazis of
Germany who had started World War II in 1939, who had
conquered and occupied the Netherlands in 1940, and who
were trying to exterminate the Jews of Europe. The Allies,
the countries fighting against Germany—among them
England, the Soviet Union, and the United States—had
reversed the Germans' early battlefield successes and were
hopeful that the terrible war would soon end. Anne was
determined to put up with the rigors of life under cover for
as long as it took the Allies to defeat the Nazis.

The Franks, the Van Daans, and Mr. Dussell had had
help in eluding detection. Hiding from the brutal German
occupation army, the Nazi police force, and informers
was possible, but it was not simply a matter of finding
an empty attic or barn and holing up inside while the
war raged beyond its walls. Far from it. The Germans
were extremely thorough in rooting out Jews and others
they considered "undesirable," such as Communists,
Gypsies, and homosexuals. Soldiers patrolled the streets
with a menacing swagger, suspicious of the slightest
peculiarity. They conducted periodic house-to-house
searches using specially trained dogs. They also relied on
a network of informers.

Occupying armies usually cannot succeed without help
from the occupied. Some of those who collaborated with
the Germans agreed with the Nazis' campaign against the
Jews. Others had decided to do whatever they felt neces-
sary in order to survive—even if that meant cooperating
with an army bent on destroying their country. Whichever
the case, it made life extremely difficult for everyone else.
How was one to know who could and could not be trusted?

At the same time, many Dutch people had defied the
Nazi authorities by forming an underground resistance

movement. They were proud of the Netherlands' tradition of tolerance and, at great risk to their lives, had taken Jews into their homes or had done other things to help protect them. Their punishment, if discovered, could be as simple and immediate as a bullet to the back of the head.

There was also the question of food and other supplies. The Franks could not possibly store enough canned food, light bulbs, toilet paper, and other necessities to last out the war. Otto Frank also wanted his daughters' education to continue and needed a constant stream of books with which to conduct their lessons. There had to be some way of replenishing their stores, some contact with the outside world, someone to see after them and be there in case of a medical emergency. Luckily, Anne and the others had several such friends: Miep Gies; her husband, Henk, who had connections to the Dutch resistance movement; Elli Vossens; Jo Koophuis, who had the main responsibility of helping the Franks and the others; and a German, Victor Kraler.

With the exception of Henk, these good people, who courageously worked together to help the Jews in hiding, were employees of Otto Frank. Frank's food-products business occupied a building at 263 Prinsengracht in Amsterdam. Nederlandsche Opekta Maatschapij N.V., or Opekta, as the company was known, was located just a few blocks west of the city's central square, where the queen's palace was also situated. Queen Wilhelmina had fled the Nazi onslaught in 1940 and had established a government-in-exile across the English Channel in Britain. From there she exhorted her compatriots, via radio, to do their best to withstand the Nazis' brutality.

Before and after the family went into hiding, Anne was a dedicated listener to these broadcasts, knowing full well that even the act of listening was considered a crime by the German occupation authorities. She also tuned in whenever news or classical music was aired. That very night, before the noise and commotion, Anne had heard one of

Above: *Miep Gies (seated) and Elli Vossens*
Right: *Jo Koophuis (left) and Victor Kraler. These four people risked their lives to help the Jews in hiding.*

her favorites, Mozart's *Eine kleine Nachtmusik* (German for "A Little Night Music"). As she later wrote of that Easter concert, "I can hardly listen in the room because I'm always so inwardly stirred when I hear lovely music."

Otto Frank had foreseen difficult times ahead for the Jews and in early 1942 had prepared a small hiding place on the second and third floors of a building behind but connected to 263 Prinsengracht. His prescience quickly proved all too accurate. The Jews of the occupied Netherlands were being rounded up and sent to death camps the Germans had erected in Germany and throughout the parts of Europe they had conquered. On July 5, 1942, Mar got Frank received a summons from the Germans ordering her to report for "working in Germany," a phrase that hid the true meaning of the summons—deportation. One day later, the Frank family left its comfortable apartment in South Amsterdam's Merwedeplein and went into hiding. Neighbors and others were led to believe that they had sought sanctuary with relatives in neutral Switzerland. The cover story seemed to have worked.

Otto Frank had trusted his employees with his secret. Non-Jews, they respected Frank as an upright businessman and honest human being. Though they faced the threat of deportation or execution for being accessories to this "crime," they had few qualms about helping in an act of resistance against the Germans. It was their duty, they felt. Thus did the Franks, Van Daans, and Mr. Dussell find the support network they needed.

A swinging door disguised as a cupboard with bookshelves separated the day-to-day business downstairs from the quiet, meager lives of the eight Jews in hiding. Downstairs, the company's work went on as usual, or at least as close to normal as the war permitted. Upstairs, during the day, the eight Jews spoke barely a word and moved around as little as possible so as not to attract any attention from Opekta customers, employees, or workmen not aware of the Jews' presence. Anne spent her days reading, writing, and napping. At night, the strictures were relaxed somewhat, and the Jews moved throughout the building, stretching their limbs, seeking privacy, all the while taking care not to betray any signs of their presence.

On the night of Easter Sunday, 1944, Peter Van Daan sneaked downstairs to investigate two loud bangs he had heard. Wartime shortages of food and work had made burglaries a constant threat. After noticing that a large plank had been removed from the door of the building, he had summoned the rest of the men. None of them had stopped to consider that by venturing so boldly out of their roost they were putting their lives in jeopardy.

When Mr. Frank, Mr. Van Daan, Mr. Dussell, and Peter Van Daan arrived downstairs, they saw thieves enlarging the hole first spotted by Peter. "Police!" shouted Mr. Van Daan, scattering the intruders. But the incident was not over. A couple walking by in the street outside, noticing

the disturbance at the building, shone a flashlight into the hole left by the burglars, illuminating the interior. The men froze and then silently moved out of the light and crept back upstairs, rejoining the women. It was now ten past ten.

As two of the men kept watch at a window overlooking the street, Otto Frank told his wife and daughters what had happened. Anne quickly realized that the true threat to their lives now came not from the burglars but from the police. Surely, she concluded, the couple with the flashlight would

Queen Wilhelmina (right) and her daughter, Princess Juliana, appear in a photo taken about six months before the Nazi invasion of the Netherlands. In 1940, the queen fled the country and established a government-in-exile in Great Britain.

report what they had seen to the police, who would in turn arrive at 263 Prinsengracht to look into the strange goings-on. This would bring an end, she feared, to their valiant attempt to survive the war. What was more, it was Easter Sunday, and Easter Monday was also a holiday. If the police were to come, they would not do so until Tuesday morning. In pitch darkness, the eight Jews settled in for an agonizing wait of two nights and a day.

At a quarter past eleven, another noise was heard downstairs—footsteps, moving from room to room and then gradually toward the secret staircase that led to the Franks' hideaway. The Jews stiffened as the trespasser—was it a policeman? a burglar? the man with the flash-light?—paused and twice rattled the swinging cupboard that covered the stairway.

"Now we are lost!" whispered Anne, as a shiver ran down her spine. She heard someone's teeth chattering. No one said a word. The rattling stopped as the cupboard refused to give way.

Then the footsteps retreated. Anne noticed that a light remained on, on the landing just beyond the cupboard. She wondered why. Had the interloper marked the secret pas-sageway? Or had he simply forgotten to turn out the light? Would someone return to put it out?

With nowhere to run, sleep was the next best escape. First, though, the families readied themselves for bed, following, as best they could, the routines of normal life. Even in hiding, stripped of all their freedom and most of their belongings, they were determined to duplicate the lives they knew before the war had sent them undercover. Unfortunately, the attempted burglary had left them no choice but to stay put in the third-floor room in which they were crowded until the "coast" could be declared clear—whenever that might be. This meant, among other things, that they would not be able to go to the washroom located on the lower of the two floors they occupied. Toilet facilities would have to be improvised.

A tin wastepaper basket would have to serve. Taking turns, the Jews relieved themselves one by one, in full sight of the others. Any embarrassment they might have felt gave way before the needs of the moment. Such lack of privacy had become, after so many months in hiding, yet another grim fact of life. When everyone had finished, Mrs. Van Daan poured some chlorine into the wastebasket and draped a towel over it in an only partially successful attempt to keep the ghastly smell from filling the room. Moments such as this impressed upon the Franks, the Van Daans, and Mr. Dussell the depths to which they had fallen since before the war. In those happier days Anne and her family had been able to walk the streets of Amsterdam proudly. Dutch society accepted them as people, and as Jews. There were no Nazis blaming the Jews for the ills of the world.

Beds were another makeshift item that night. Anne, for example, was stretched out on the floor, positioned between the legs of a table, her feet serving as a pillow first for Mrs. and then Mr. Van Daan. Meanwhile, the Jews' nervousness had hardly subsided.

Everyone continued whispering well past midnight, speculating uneasily about what might happen next. Fearing that they would be interrogated by the Gestapo, the German secret police, they considered making an attempt to escape.

Ultimately, Anne later related, the talk turned to bravery. As she told Mrs. Van Daan, "We must behave like soldiers. . . . If all is up now, then let's go for Queen and Country, for freedom, truth, and the right, as they always say on the Dutch News from England. The only thing that is really rotten is that we get a lot of other people into trouble, too."

Anne was referring to Miep and the others who had helped them. The discovery of the two-story hiding place would brand them as collaborators, that much was certain. What more evidence did the Germans need than a secret

The entrance to the hiding place, which Anne called the Secret Annex, was concealed by a movable cupboard with bookshelves. Just inside the swinging door was a steep staircase that led to the third floor, the living quarters.

door disguised as a cupboard-bookshelf and, behind it, eight Jews? But there was even more evidence, and it existed in a most incriminating way: in writing.

On June 12, 1942, Anne had been given a diary for her 13th birthday. She began keeping a record of her life, filling the volume with observations, accounts of her school days, and reports on her family and on events in the occupied Netherlands. Less than a month later, the Franks slipped away from their Amsterdam apartment and into their hiding place. Anne continued making detailed diary entries. Names, dates—all of this and more was included. Though to her the diary was a private, highly personal document for her eyes only, to the Germans it could be used as convincing proof of "treason" on the part of Miep, Henk, and the others.

The Jews considered the problem of the diary for a moment as they tried to fall asleep. Mrs. Van Daan offered a suggestion: "Burn it." A horrified Anne, as frightened as when the swinging cupboard seemed about to give way, was swift to respond: "Not my diary; if my diary goes, I go with it!" Otto Frank, knowing how much the diary meant to his daughter, did not reply, and talk progressed to other matters.

The next few hours passed slowly. At seven in the morning it was decided to phone Mr. Koophuis to let him know what had happened. Despite the risk involved—the phone might be heard if someone was still downstairs—the risk of not phoning was considered greater. A short time later, loud footsteps could be heard downstairs.

"That's Henk," said Anne. "No, no, it's the police," said some of the others. Anne watched as a terrified Mrs. Van Daan turned white as a sheet and collapsed into a chair. She had almost fainted.

There was a knock on the swinging cupboard, then a whistle. The Jews at the top of the stairs erupted in shouts and tears as Miep and Henk let themselves into the hiding place. A tearful Anne threw her arms around Miep, whose heart was still thumping from rushing over to 263 Prinsengracht after hearing from Mr. Koophuis. Everyone spoke at once, relating the awful events of the previous night.

Miep helped the family clean up the evening's mess as, one by one, the Jews visited the bathroom on the lower floor to wash, brush their teeth, and tidy themselves. Henk, meanwhile, fixed the hole in the door on the ground floor. Then he came upstairs to deliver a stern warning: "Stay behind the bookcase, no matter what. If you hear something, never go. Be silent, wait. Never go." He went on to remind them that people in hiding were caught not so much because of informers but because of mistakes they themselves made. They should not, he told them, grow complacent about their situation. They could not afford to forget that their lives were in danger every moment of the day.

Henk also had some good news. The person on the landing had been the night watchman, Mr. Slagter. He had noticed the hole made by the burglars and had inspected the building accompanied by a policeman. Evidently, this was as close as the police would come to the hiding place. In addition, the person who had shone a flashlight into the building during the course of the burglary was the local greengrocer. This man had elected not to say anything to the police, telling Henk, "I don't know anything, but I guess a lot." Apparently, he suspected that someone was hiding at 263 Prinsengracht but was holding his tongue—another good Dutch citizen doing his part for the anti-German resistance.

The scare had passed, but not without some soul-searching on the part of Anne. As she wrote in her diary a few days later: "Who has inflicted this upon us? . . . Who has allowed us to suffer so terribly up till now? . . . God has never deserted our people. Right through the ages there have been Jews, through all the ages they have had to suffer, but it has made them strong too; the weak fall, but the strong will remain and never go under!"

Very few teenage girls have to learn such lessons or confront the cruel facts of persecution and genocide—the systematic killing of a whole people or nation. But as Anne had discovered, these were exceptional times. Europe and the rest of the world were convulsed in a deadly war. A powerful madman, Adolf Hitler, was using the most barbaric means imaginable to lead his nation, Germany, to his professed goal of world domination. Would the young woman hiding in the tiny attic survive?

Margot (right) looks at one-month-old Anne in July 1929. This photo was taken by Otto Frank, who was a keen amateur photographer.

2

The Rise of Nazi Germany

ANNELIESE MARIE FRANK WAS BORN on June 12, 1929. Anne, as she was called, was the second child of Otto and Edith (Holländer) Frank, who had been married in the spring of 1925. The Franks' first daughter, Margot Betti, was born on February 16, 1926.

The family lived in a five-room apartment on Ganghoferstrasse in Frankfurt, Germany, and could trace its roots in the city back to the 17th century. The Franks enjoyed a generally comfortable middle-class life, and in the relatively liberal social climate of Frankfurt their circle of friends included Jews and non-Jews alike.

But the 1920s and early 1930s were a time of unprecedented turmoil and uncertainty in Germany. The most immediate upheaval had been caused by the Great Depression, which began just a few months after Anne was born. Sparked in the United States by the Wall Street stock market crash of October 1929, the depression triggered a decade of worldwide economic hardship. Among the many millions to suffer from the crisis was Otto Frank.

Otto Frank had gotten involved in business quite early in life. In 1909, at the age of 20, he dropped out of the prestigious University of Heidelberg to accompany a fellow student to New York City. That

*Berliners wait their turn
on a soup line during the
Great Depression of the
1930s. The Bankgeschäft
Michael Frank was hit hard
by the financial crisis, and
in March 1933, Otto Frank
decided it was time to close
its doors.*

student was Nathan Straus, whose family owned R. H. Macy, the world's largest department store. Frank made several trips to the bustling metropolis, receiving something of a crash course in running a business, and he also worked in Düsseldorf for a few years. During World War I, he served as a lieutenant in an artillery regiment. Then he decided to go into the family business: banking.

The Bankgeschäft (banking house) Michael Frank had been founded in 1885 and was named after Otto Frank's father. Otto Frank joined the bank in the early 1920s, several years after Michael Frank's death, not so much out of an interest in banking as a sense of filial responsibility: The family business was in trouble.

World War I had plagued the Bankgeschäft Michael Frank with the disastrous combination of inflation, debt, and restrictive legislation. But if Otto Frank thought the postwar years would bring a reversal of fortune, he was mistaken. First came the failure of a foreign-currency trading venture in Amsterdam. Then came an unfortunate incident involving Otto Frank's younger brother, Herbert, who also worked at the bank. The bank became the target of an anonymous complaint denouncing one of its financial dealings. Given the long history of anti-Semitism in Germany and the laws enacted against them, Jews were frequently the victims of unscrupulous people who falsely accused them of wrongdoing. The incident prompted criminal charges and left a stain on the bank's name. By the early 1930s, with the depression in full swing, it had become apparent to Otto Frank that the bank could not survive. In March 1933, he closed its doors for good.

That month was auspicious for another reason: It marked the full rise to power of a German dictator named Adolf Hitler. Hitler was the head of the National Socialist German Workers, or Nazi, party and portrayed himself as a forceful leader devoted to the creation of a powerful German state. In Germany's desperate, unstable years following World War I, it was an image with great appeal.

One reason for Hitler's burgeoning popularity was that Germans were indignant at the treatment their country had received at the Versailles Peace Conference of 1919, which had been called to put a formal end to the conflict. The Treaty of Versailles cited Germany as solely responsible for the devastating war, stripped it of many valuable overseas colonies, and demanded payment of reparations—all under threat of invasion by the victorious Allies, among them France, Great Britain, Italy, and the United States.

Hitler's promises to provide jobs for all and to redistribute the nation's wealth also brought him new followers during a period of skyrocketing inflation and widespread unemployment. At the same time, fractious politics and the threat of a Communist revolution bankrolled by the Communist leadership of the Soviet Union made many German citizens long for a government that had more authority to cope with the country's many problems.

Hitler was a riveting, charismatic speaker, and in his many public addresses he emphasized German nationalism, anticommunism, the supremacy of the German "race," and the need for order and security. The combination made for effective politics.

After the elections of 1932, the Nazis became the largest party in the Reichstag, or German parliament. In January 1933, Hitler was appointed chancellor. In March 1933, the Nazis won an electoral majority in the Reichstag, which subsequently voted to dissolve itself and grant Hitler dictatorial powers.

Many Germans were frightened by the astonishing rise of Adolf Hitler. Much of Europe, too, and, indeed, the civilized world in general, saw him as a threat to the peace. Central to his tactics and beliefs were extremely violent attacks based on race.

Hitler advanced racist views declaring the Germans, or Aryans, as he called them, a "pure" and "master" race destined to rule the world. He spoke of expanding

In 1916, Otto Frank (right) poses with his brother, Herbert, when Otto was a lieutenant in the German army. During World War I, Frank served in an artillery regiment.

Germany's borders to encompass much of Poland and the Soviet Union and of forcing the "subhuman" Slavic inhabitants of those countries to serve as slaves.

But it was the Jews who were singled out by Hitler for his most vitriolic sentiments. He claimed repeatedly that the Jews were a "cancer" that had "soiled" Germany. He said they were an inferior race responsible for all of society's troubles, including communism. Put simply, he said, they were a constant threat to Germany and should be destroyed, exterminated, wiped off the face of the earth. These racist beliefs had been part of Hitler's message ever since he first became leader of the Nazi party in 1921. Now, as leader of all Germany, he put anti-Jewish measures into effect with the full force of law.

Among his first acts as dictator was to put under government control all forms of communications—books, newspapers, radios, and motion pictures—in a comprehensive propaganda effort aimed at molding public opinion to his point of view. Any kind of protest or dissent was punished by arrests, beatings, and torture by the Gestapo, the secret police.

Jews—who were defined as anyone with a Jewish grandparent or who had married a Jew—immediately felt the brunt of harassment as specific targets of the new German regime. They were dismissed from government jobs. They were not allowed to work in the media or in the schools. Shops refused to sell them food and other goods, and hotels would not give them rooms. Their children were separated from Aryan classmates. Orthodox Jews who had grown long beards and sidelocks as a sign of religious adherence had their hair scissored in public by Nazi storm troopers, who egged each other on in humiliating them. For the Jews, this was only the beginning of more than a decade of sheer terror. Anti-Semitism proved to be a very useful tool of Hitler's propaganda. Hitler had initiated what was later called his "Final Solution" to the "Jewish problem."

In 1935, Adolf Hitler, his hand raised in the Nazi salute, reviews thousands of Hitler Youth in the stadium in Nuremberg. When the German government failed to solve the nation's economic crisis, the people were ready to accept any solution that offered an end to their problems. Hitler's Third Reich began in 1933, when he became chancellor.

A Jewish boy is forced to cut his father's beard while Nazi soldiers look on mockingly. Anti-Semitism was not new in Germany, but under the Hitler regime Jews became the specific targets of hatred.

Sadly, too, it was far from the first time in history that the Jews had been victims of hatred. Their entire history, dating back thousands of years, is rife with episodes of violence committed against them. The most memorable examples from ancient times were the destruction of two glorious temples in Jerusalem.

The first was built by King Solomon in the 10th century B.C. It became the center of Jewish religious worship and the symbol of an empire that stretched throughout ancient Palestine, which encompassed today's Israel and parts of Lebanon, Syria, Jordan, and Egypt. The temple was razed by the Babylonians in 586 B.C., and the Jews were dispersed; most were taken to Babylonia to serve as slaves. The settlement of the Jews outside of Palestine is referred to by Jews as the Diaspora. In A.D. 66–70, the Romans destroyed a second temple built during a resurgence of Jewish power in the Holy Land. Once again the Jews were driven into exile. Always, they pledged to return.

Anti-Semitism, the systematic oppression of Jews as a religious or racial group, was prevalent in Europe throughout the Middle Ages (roughly, the period from the late 5th through the late 15th centuries). In Christian Europe, Jews were scorned and persecuted in the belief that they were responsible for the crucifixion of Jesus Christ.

Nicolas Poussin's painting The Destruction of Jerusalem by the Romans *depicts the razing of the Jewish Temple in* A.D. *66–70. The systematic oppression of Jews dates back thousands of years.*

The Crusades, a series of Christian military expeditions that sought to "liberate" the Holy Land from the Muslim "infidels" who ruled the region, led to a wave of massacres against the Jews. The first Crusade was launched in the late 11th century; the military marches were held periodically over the next several hundred years. Historians have said the massacres occurred in part because of heightened religious passions at the time.

The Spanish Inquisition also prompted the slaughter of Jews. This was an intensely violent campaign against suspected religious "heretics" that was established in 1478 by King Ferdinand and Queen Isabella of Spain. The Jews were hated largely because many had become financiers who were influential with the Spanish court. This made them an easy target of the wrath of non-Jewish citizens oppressed by taxes or other economic hardships.

Anti-Semitism plagued Germany, Poland, and Russia throughout the ensuing centuries for many of the same reasons.

In 19th- and 20th-century Russia, for example, Jews were forced to live in a region along the country's western frontier known as the Pale of Settlement. About 5 million Jews lived there in poverty, facing the constant threat of persecution and massacres, known as pogroms, carried out by Russian soldiers and citizens alike. (The word *pale* is a noun meaning an area having certain bounds. Since the days of the Pale of Settlement, the phrase *beyond the pale* has come into use; it refers to actions or behavior considered outside established norms.)

Some countries were relatively free of official anti-Semitism. In England, Benjamin Disraeli, a Jew, had served twice as prime minister. France, meanwhile, was considered among the more enlightened and liberal countries in Europe. Imagine the Jews' shock over the case of a Jewish army officer named Alfred Dreyfus. In the 1890s, Dreyfus was convicted of treason for passing military information to the Germans and condemned to life imprisonment on Devil's Island in French Guiana. In 1906, a court set aside the Dreyfus decision as "wrongful" and "erroneous" and acknowledged that the actions against Dreyfus could be traced to anti-Semitism. But by then the

Victims of a pogrom in Russia in 1919.

In France during the
1890s, Captain Alfred
Dreyfus (standing, fourth
from right) was wrongfully
convicted of treason for
passing military informa-
tion to the Germans. Before
the Dreyfus affair, most
Jews had considered
France one of the more
enlightened and liberal
countries in Europe.

damage had been done. If such blatant anti-Semitism existed in France, the Jews reasoned, they were not safe anywhere.

Theodor Herzl, the Paris correspondent for a Viennese newspaper, had covered the Dreyfus court proceedings and witnessed mobs shouting, "Death to the Jews." He concluded that the only way that the Jews could ever hope to live in freedom and with dignity would be if they had a state of their own. In 1896, he published a pamphlet called *Der Judenstaat* (The Jewish State), giving birth to the modern Zionist movement and sparking the repopulation of Palestine by Jews hoping to create a new nation in their biblical homeland. (Zion is the name given in the Old Testament of the Bible to the city of the Jewish King David and is symbolic of the Jewish desire to establish their homeland in the Holy Land.)

The knowledge that suffering had been their lot for thousands of years did little to assuage the horror Jews felt now as they listened to Hitler's tirades against the Jews. Otto Frank was distraught at what had happened to the cultured German society he had known—and of which he had considered himself a part. He knew that Anne and Margot would have no future if the family remained in Germany and quickly concluded that emigration was the only choice. He also realized that the Franks would have to leave the country as soon as possible. There was no telling how much longer Jews would be granted permission to do so.

His choice of destination was fairly obvious. Otto Frank was familiar with the Netherlands's long-standing and deserved tradition as a place of refuge for Jews and others facing discrimination or other troubles in their home countries. He also knew Amsterdam relatively well, having traveled there several times on business. Finally, he had received a job offer from his brother-in-law, Erich Elias. Elias had worked with Otto and Herbert Frank in the Bankgeschäft Michael Frank but left in 1929 to open a Swiss branch of Opekta-Werke, a subsidiary of the Frankfurt Pomosin-Werke. Opekta, a manufacturer and distributor of pectin, a gelling agent used in jams and jellies, wanted to open a retail branch of the company in Amsterdam. Elias asked Otto Frank if he would be interested in the position.

In the summer of 1933, the Franks left Frankfurt for Aachen, Edith's hometown. Edith, Margot, and Anne remained there with Edith's family while Otto went on ahead to Amsterdam to set up the business and find living quarters. A slight hitch in the work arrangements led Otto to set up his own independent food-products business using the Opekta trademark, with the help of a loan from his brother-in-law. He then found an apartment on the second floor of a building at 37 Merwedeplein, a quiet little square in the southern part of the city. Edith and Margot joined Otto in December. Anne arrived in March 1934. The Franks were reunited and ready to begin anew.

Edith Holländer and Otto Frank visited San Remo, Italy, on their honeymoon in 1925. Through his brother-in-law, Otto set up a retail branch of Opekta-Werke, a food processing business, in Amsterdam in 1933.

Anne and Margot pose for a photograph around 1933. A family friend remembered Anne as a quiet four-year-old—but this was not surprising because Anne was just beginning to learn to speak Dutch.

3

No Refuge for the Jews

ANNE FRANK LOVED HER NEW HOME in Amsterdam and was very content with her life there. As she wrote later, while in hiding, "Oh how I wish that those happy, carefree days could come again!"

Amsterdam was a city in which Jews were prominent in the worlds of culture, commerce, and politics. It was home to about 80,000 Jews, roughly 60 percent of the country's total Jewish population of 140,000. They formed an integral part of the fabric of city life and, perhaps most important to them, were treated as equals.

Otto Frank worked hard at building up his business. Edith worked as a homemaker and was involved in Jewish community affairs. Anne and Margot entered school.

Though Margot was considered the better student, Anne was the "social butterfly" of the family, as a neighbor later recalled. Anne had lots of friends, was a follower of the latest fashions, and was an avid reader of movie magazines. Even as a youngster she was considered

In 1935, Anne (seated at back, center) attended a Montessori school. The Montessori method of educating small children is based on the theory that a child will learn naturally if given "learning games" suited to his or her interests. The method relies on self-motivation, and the teacher intervenes only when a child needs help.

stylish and sophisticated for her age, which may explain why she was so popular with boys, and they with her. A slender young girl with thick brown hair falling just shy of her shoulders, she also possessed a sweetly serious countenance and intelligent dark eyes that communicated a sense of mature purpose even amid the passing fancies of youth.

Another family friend remembered Anne as a quiet four-year-old, which is not surprising; at that age she had just begun to learn to speak Dutch. By the age of nine, however, she was renowned for her rapid-fire delivery—especially in class. At one point her outbursts earned her a series of after-school writing assignments as punishment. The first, she was told by her teacher, should be called "A Chatterbox." The second was to be called "An Incorrigible Chatterbox." The third—and by now the teacher seemed to be having a bit of a joke with Anne—was to be titled

"'Quack, quack,' said Mrs. Quackenbush." Anne took her punishment good-naturedly, crafting rhymes where other students might be more apt to scrawl "I will not talk" 100 times. No more essays were assigned after the third one, but the nickname—Mrs. Quackenbush—stuck.

Anne's parents also encouraged her to write. A steady stream of letters and postcards were sent to friends and relatives abroad to commemorate birthdays, anniversaries, and other occasions. At home the Franks celebrated the Jewish Sabbath, the day of rest that begins with the lighting of candles at sundown on Friday and ends at sundown on Saturday, as well as other Jewish holidays, such as Passover, which commemorates the Jews' exodus from slavery in Egypt during biblical times.

Even as they honored the Jewish traditions, the Franks had come to feel increasingly at home in the Netherlands, and the children were becoming more and more Dutch through their schooling and new friendships. This effort to

On her 10th birthday, Anne (second from left) poses with her girlfriends. Anne had many friends, followed the latest fashions, and eagerly read movie magazines.

achieve a balance between their Jewish identity and the larger, non-Jewish society in which they lived was a challenge well known to Jews. Through much of their long history, Jews had lived as a minority, dependent on the tolerance of a host country. The Netherlands had extended what many historians have said was an exemplary welcome to the Jews. Germany had once shown something of the same character, but things there had taken a horrible turn for the worse.

In 1935, the Nazis adopted the Nuremberg Laws, which legitimized anti-Jewish discrimination and violence and brought about the final disfranchisement of the Jews of Germany. On the night of November 9–10, 1938, Hitler's storm troopers sacked and burned homes, synagogues, and shops owned by Jews, and beat and arrested vast numbers of people. This night of rampage and wanton violence has come to be known as *Kristallnacht*, or Crystal Night, for all the shattered glass that littered the German streets.

By this time, most of the countries of Europe were also trembling with fear. People everywhere anticipated another large-scale outbreak of war. Many asked how the countries of Europe had failed to learn any lessons from World War I. But their plaints were mere whispers before the ambitions of Adolf Hitler.

Earlier in 1938, Hitler had sent his army into Austria and Czechoslovakia to assert and establish German control over those countries. In September, he and English prime minister Neville Chamberlain signed the Munich Pact, which committed Germany to ending its aggression toward Czechoslovakia in exchange for assuming control of the Sudetenland, a region of that country with a large German population. However, statesmen everywhere believed that Germany would not honor the agreement. Indeed, historians say that the Munich Pact only served to feed Germany's appetite for territory and power and was a prime example of national weakness. IN MUNICH HONOR DIED, read the headline in several English newspapers.

In August 1939, the Soviet Union and Germany announced that they had signed a nonaggression pact. This was, in fact, cause for alarm because it was commonly understood that the Soviet Union and Germany both coveted pieces of Polish territory, making full-fledged war imminent. Sure enough, on September 1, 1939, Germany invaded Poland and Nazi bombs rained down on Warsaw, the Polish capital. Two days later, France and Great Britain declared war on Germany. World War II had begun.

The Netherlands had declared its neutrality during the summer of 1938. Otto Frank believed the Nazis would respect this claim. But on May 10, 1940, he was proved wrong, as Germany invaded the tiny country in a blizzard of air raids, paratroopers, tanks, and artillery fire. Queen Wilhelmina fled on a ship to England, taking with her all the gold from the Dutch treasury. The Germans, meanwhile, bombed Rotterdam to bits and threatened to do the same to Amsterdam if the country refused to capitulate. The Netherlands had no choice but to surrender. On May 14, 1940, the fifth day of the invasion, the German army marched through Amsterdam's Dam Square and hoisted its national flag in place of the Netherlands's. In the coming weeks, Luxembourg, Belgium, and the city of Paris, France, fell in swift succession. There seemed, at least for the time being, no resisting the force of the Nazis' armaments. Dutch Jews were particularly concerned. They felt it would be only a matter of time before Nuremberg-like strictures were put into place.

They were right. In The Hague, the Dutch government seat located just 35 miles south of Amsterdam, signs reading Jews Not Wanted and Not for Jews began to appear on park benches and in other public places. A series of edicts issued by the German high commissioner of the Netherlands, Arthur Seyss-Inquart, banned Jews from cinemas, restaurants, hotels, libraries, public swimming pools, buses, and streetcars. Jews were dismissed from teaching jobs and the civil service and forbidden to practice

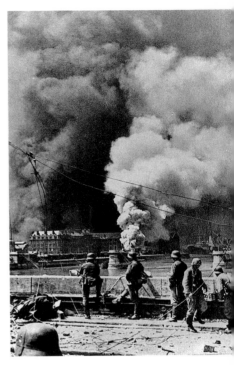

On May 14, 1940, German soldiers watched Rotterdam go up in flames after the city was bombed by the German air force. Germany invaded the Netherlands four days earlier, and the Dutch army surrendered on May 14.

many other professions. Jewish businesses and property were confiscated. Non-Jewish doctors and dentists were prohibited from treating Jews. Fights between Jews and the Nazis who harassed them broke out in the streets. Protests by non-Jewish Dutch citizens against the anti-Jewish actions were violently suppressed. All Jews were forced to register with the German authorities—the first step in what would later become a ruthlessly efficient deportation program.

Children were not exempt from the Nazis' attention. In August 1941, a decree barred Jews from Dutch public schools and vocational schools. Following the summer vacation from school in 1941, Anne was forced to attend the Jewish Lyceum, where all the teachers and students were Jewish.

Miep Gies remembers Anne being deeply affected by the harsh new realities of life as a Jew in the occupied Netherlands. As she wrote in her memoirs, *Anne Frank Remembered*, "[Anne] was very indignant about the injustices being heaped on the Jewish people. . . . It was as though the terrible events in the outside world were speeding up this little girl's development, as though Anne were suddenly in a hurry to know and experience everything.

A collection of Stars of David from various countries. The Nazis required all Jews to wear an identifying yellow star printed with the word Jood *(Dutch for "Jew") or* Jude *(German for "Jew").*

On the outside, Anne was a delicate, vivacious . . . girl, but on the inside, a part of her was suddenly much older."

But in her own testimony, Anne reveals no such gravity. Rather, her memories of the days she spent at the Jewish Lyceum are happy, more like schoolgirl giddiness at its most typical. "When we still were part of ordinary, everyday life, everything was just marvelous," she wrote. "That one year in the Lyceum was sheer bliss for me; the teachers, all that they taught me, the jokes, the prestige, the romances, and the adoring boys."

Among Anne's closest childhood friends was Lies Goosens, whose family had also fled Nazi Germany and settled on the Merwedeplein. The two families became friendly and celebrated holidays together. The two girls, who were the same age, went through school in the same classes and did their homework together on Sundays.

Once, at the Lyceum, the girls' togetherness went a little too far, at least in the eyes of their French teacher. During a test, an unprepared Lies copied from Anne, who knew the material well. The girls were caught cheating and given zeros. But in the course of their interrogation by the teacher Lies blurted out, in front of the entire class, that nearly everyone had had their books open under their desks. A day or two later the teacher surprised the class by giving the test all over again. As Anne later recalled, she and Lies were "cut dead" as traitors.

Again putting her writing talent to good use, a 12-year-old Anne crafted a letter of apology that read, in part, "Anne Frank and Lies Goosens herewith offer the pupils of Class 16 II their sincere apologies for the cowardly betrayal. . . . It was an unpremeditated, thoughtless act, and we admit without hesitation that we are the only ones who should have been punished." Within two weeks, the incident was forgotten.

Though absorbed in her schoolwork and blossoming friendships at the Jewish Lyceum, Anne also stayed very much attuned to the progress of the war. She was a devoted listener of Radio Orange, the Dutch broadcasts from England. (Orange is the Netherlands' national color.) The same autumn that Anne entered the Jews-only school, the radio was filled with reports of a spreading conflict.

In June 1941, seeking to establish himself as the supreme power on the European continent, Hitler sent his army to attack the Soviet Union. But the Germans met surprisingly stiff resistance and by December were forced to lift their siege of Moscow and retreat. Also in December, the war became truly global in scope with Japan's attack on the U.S. naval base at Pearl Harbor, Hawaii. The Japanese had allied themselves with Germany. The United States quickly entered the war on the side of England, France, and the other European victims of Hitler.

These developments promised new heights of hardship and destruction. But in many ways the news was also uplifting. In attacking Russia, it was thought, Hitler had finally overreached. For the first time his army had been stopped. Meanwhile, the United States, with all its manpower and arms, had entered the fight against Hitler.

In the Netherlands, conditions continued to worsen. Jews who lived outside of Amsterdam were being stripped of their homes and possessions and forced into the city. Food was being rationed, and Jews had to shop between 3:00 P.M. and 5:00 P.M. in "Jewish" shops only. A curfew dictated that Jews could not venture outdoors, not even into their gardens, after 8:00 P.M.

Otto Frank entertained little hope that the war would soon end nor any illusions about the direction things were going in for the Jews. On January 20, 1942, he appears to have made an attempt to initiate emigration proceedings for the family by submitting the appropriate form to the Emigration Section of the Amsterdam Jewish Council. The form was discovered after the war. It is not clear exactly what came of the effort, but the Franks remained in Amsterdam.

Dutch Jews at Westerbork prepare to be transported to Auschwitz. On the afternoon of July 5, 1942, Margot Frank was ordered to report "for work" in Germany.

On April 29, 1942, a Nazi decree was issued requiring all Jews to wear an identifying yellow star printed with the word *Jood* (Dutch for "Jew"). The six-pointed star was to be sewn onto clothing above the heart. If a Jew wanted to take off his or her outer coat, he or she had to have sewn a yellow star on the shirt or blouse beneath in order to avoid being liable for arrest.

One morning shortly after this latest and most humiliating edict, Otto Frank called Miep into his private office. "I have a secret to confide to you," he told Miep. "Edith, Margot, Anne, and I are planning to go under—to go into hiding. . . . Are you willing to take on the responsibility of taking care of us while we are in hiding?"

"Of course," replied Miep. As Miep later wrote, "There is a look between two people once or twice in a lifetime that cannot be described by words. That look passed between us."

"Miep," said Otto, "For those who help Jews, the punishment is harsh; imprisonment, perhaps—"

"I said, 'Of course.' I meant it."

"Good. Only Koophuis knows. Even Margot and Anne do not know yet."

But even as Otto Frank was readying his family's hiding place, the Nazis were making preparations of their own. Two transit camps, Westerbork and Vught, were set up where Jews would be kept until they could be shipped by train to the death camp at Auschwitz in Poland. In July 1942, the deportations began, and Margot Frank was among the first to be summoned. On the afternoon of July 5 she received a postcard ordering her to report for work in Germany.

When Anne found out, she grew frightened and began to cry. She could not believe that the Germans could be so merciless as to take young girls away to a concentration camp. Just that morning she had learned from her father that the family planned to go into hiding. Anne tried to ask where, and when, but her father was not ready to divulge his plans. "Don't you worry about it, we shall arrange everything. Make the most of your carefree young life while you can," her father replied. Just hours later, that carefree, young way of life came to an end.

Anne and Margot began to gather their belongings. As she later wrote in the diary she had received for her 13th birthday, celebrated less than a month earlier, "The first

Anne (left) and her sister, Margot, posed for these photos in May 1942, two months before they were forced to go into hiding in Amsterdam. Although Otto Frank did not tell his daughters about their hiding place until that July, he had already been secretly preparing the living quarters for several months.

thing I put in [the suitcase] was this diary, then hair curlers, handkerchiefs, schoolbooks, a comb, old letters; I put in the craziest things with the idea that we were going into hiding. But I'm not sorry, memories mean more to me than dresses."

Miep and her husband, Henk, hurried to the Frank household after Otto Frank telephoned and told them the bad news. They made two trips to the hiding place carrying clothing the family would need. The next morning, Anne and the others donned layer upon layer of clothing so they could bring still more into hiding; a Jew in the street carrying a suitcase would have been a suspicious sight.

Though it was July, Anne wore two pairs of stockings, three pairs of pants, a dress, a skirt, two vests, a jacket, a summer coat, a woolly cap, a scarf, and more. At 7:30 in the morning, Anne said farewell to her apartment, went out into the rain, and girded herself for the two-and-a-half-mile walk. Jews were banned from public transport, and the yellow stars the Franks wore meant that no one in passing cars would give them a lift.

During the walk Anne learned from her father about the hiding place he had prepared. For several months, he told her, he had fixed up the empty upper floors of 263 Prinsengracht with furniture, supplies, and some of the Franks' belongings. He had hoped to have the place fully ready by July 16, but the Nazi summons had forced the family to move 10 days early.

Anne surveyed her new home at 263 Prinsengracht in a state of bewilderment. The unfamiliar surroundings; the idea that this was to be their home, indefinitely; and the sight of boxes waiting to be unpacked—it was a lot to take in all at once. But she knew that the family had to make the best of it all if they were to successfully wait out the war. As she wrote, "Mummy and Margot . . . were tired and lay down on their beds, they were miserable, and lots more besides. But the two 'clearers-up' of the family— Daddy and myself—wanted to start at once."

The Franks' hiding place, which Anne called the Secret Annex, was located behind the building of 263 Prinsengracht and was connected to the building by a narrow passageway and a steep staircase on the second floor.

4

The Secret Annex

ONE DAY SOON AFTER ANNE and her family had gone into hiding, Lies Goosens went over to the Franks' apartment. Surprised to find her close friend and schoolmate gone, she asked a neighbor what had happened. "Don't you know," she was told, "that the entire Frank family has gone to Switzerland?"

The Franks had made no secret of their having relatives in Switzerland. This served as a perfect cover story, and the answer Lies received showed that it was working. Actually, the Franks had considered inviting Lies and her family into hiding with them. But Lies had a two-year-old sister, and her mother was pregnant. The crying of two infants, it was felt, would jeopardize the secrecy of the hiding place, and so the Goosens had to fend for themselves.

But because there was additional room at 263 Prinsengracht, another family joined the Franks in the upstairs quarters. On July 13, 1942, the Van Daans—Hermann, a colleague of Otto Frank's at work; his wife,

Petronella; and his 16-year-old son, Peter—"disappeared" behind the swinging cupboard. With their belongings they brought news of what had happened in the week since the Franks had vanished. Anne laughed when she heard that one neighbor claimed to have seen the Franks taken away by a military vehicle in the middle of the night.

In November, another Jew in need of a place to hide joined the Franks and Van Daans: Albert Dussell, Miep's dentist. A few days after confiding in her about his desperate situation, Dussell was brought to 263 Prinsengracht and led upstairs. When he beheld Otto Frank, he turned pale, as if he had seen a ghost. Dussell, too, had thought the Franks were no longer in Amsterdam.

Anne's name for the eight Jews' living quarters was the "Secret Annex," and she was quick to see the virtues of her new circumstances. As she wrote in her diary during her first week inside:

> I don't think I shall ever feel really at home in this house,
> but that does not mean that I loathe it here. It is more like
> being on vacation in a very peculiar boardinghouse.
> Rather a mad idea, perhaps, but that is how it strikes me.
> The 'Secret Annex' is an ideal hiding place. Although it
> leans to one side and is damp, you'd never find such a
> comfortable hiding place anywhere in Amsterdam, no,
> perhaps not even in the whole of Holland.

The backyard building that housed the Secret Annex was built in 1635 and was near the Prinsengracht, one of the main canals in a city famous for its canals. On one side was another building filled with offices; on the other was a furniture workshop. The ground floor served as a warehouse. The first floor and the front part of the second floor served as office and storage space for Otto Frank's food-products business. During the day, Miep, Mr. Koophuis, Elli Vossens, and other employees worked in the large, light front office while Mr. Kraler occupied the

rear office. Prior to his "disappearance," Hermann Van Daan had shared this space with Kraler.

A small storeroom between the two offices housed a safe. At the rear of the floor, at the end of a long passageway, were a kitchen and a well-appointed private office previously used by Otto Frank. A wooden staircase connected the first floor with a second-floor landing. To one side of the landing and down a narrow passageway was a door leading to the storerooms that occupied the front portion of the floor. The other side of the landing was marked by the swinging cupboard.

Otto Frank had a food-products business on the first floor and part of the second floor of 263 Prinsengracht (center), situated next to the Prinsengracht Canal.

This staircase leads from the swinging cupboard to the third floor of the Secret Annex.

Just inside the cupboard-cum-door, on the right, was a steep staircase to the third floor. To the left of the staircase, through a door, was a small room that served as Mr. and Mrs. Franks' bedroom. To the right of the staircase was a windowless area containing a washbasin and, behind a door, a toilet. A door from this area led to another small room that was first used as Margot's and Anne's bedroom. After Mr. Dussell arrived, he and Anne shared this space while Margot slept on a folding cot in her parents' bedroom. Anne was somewhat wary of this stranger at first, but as she wrote, "One must be prepared to make some sacrifices for a good cause, so I shall make my little offering with a good will."

The main room on the third floor was the Secret Annex's bright surprise. Large and light, by day it served as the Jews' living room, dining room, and kitchen, and at night it became a bedroom for Mr. and Mrs. Van Daan. The gas stove had been connected on this floor so that any cooking noises would not be heard by customers or workers downstairs. A corridor room off the kitchen served as Peter Van Daan's bedroom. A staircase led from this small space to the building's attic.

Windows at the rear of the second and third floors looked out onto adjacent buildings, but the eight Jews had to be extremely careful about taking in even this meager view so as not to be seen by a neighbor or worker in what were supposedly storerooms. One of those nearby buildings was the Westerkerk, a church, the clocktower bells of which chimed every quarter hour, reverberating through the rooms day and night. Anne thought of the clock as her "faithful friend," but some of the others had difficulty adjusting to its presence, especially during the early morning hours. As the war intensified, another noise became Anne's constant companion: the roar and drone of airplanes—German bombers raining further destruction on the Netherlands and then, later in the war, Allied planes on their way to bomb Germany.

The eight Jews quickly settled into a routine of quiet days and nights. Everyone was to speak softly at all times and move around as little as possible. Breakfast was at 9:00 A.M. during the week and at 11:30 A.M. on Sundays, and lunch was from 1:15 P.M. to 1:45 P.M.. Dinnertime was flexible, depending on the daily news broadcasts. At the end of the typical working day, when everyone else had gone home, Anne and the others would sneak downstairs to listen to Radio Orange or the British Broadcasting Service (BBC) for updates on the war. Since it was illegal for Jews to have radios and to listen to these stations, they had to remember not to leave the dial set to these frequencies. Later the Jews were given a radio of their own. Anne also listened to classical music broadcasts—the only time she would tune in to a German station. Anne livened up her bedroom walls by pasting up pictures—an Opekta advertisement, a drawing of chimpanzees having a tea party, a copy of Michelangelo's *Pietà*, cutouts of babies, and photos of movie stars—among them Greta Garbo, Ray Milland, Ginger Rogers, and Norma Shearer. Miep Gies remembers that Anne liked to talk about movie stars and would do so with anyone willing to listen.

In her bedroom in the Secret Annex, Anne decorated the walls with pictures of movies stars, cutouts of babies, and a drawing of chimpanzees having a tea party.

Anne Frank's diary and other writings. Anne once wrote about a typical day in the Secret Annex, beginning at nine in the evening with the bedtime preparations, which included putting up the blackout curtains.

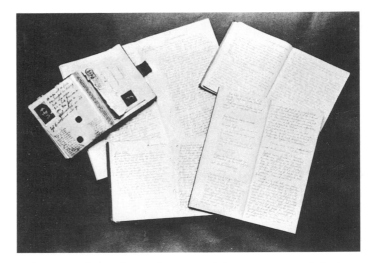

Lessons formed a major part of the young people's day. Under the supervision of Otto Frank, Anne, Margot, and Peter were taught English, French, math, and history. Anne and Margot also took lessons in shorthand, courtesy of a correspondence course in which Elli Vossens had enrolled. Elli and Miep also left office work for Margot and Anne. At night the sisters would sneak downstairs to the back offices, and Miep and Elli would find the filing and invoicing finished when they arrived for work the next morning.

On her own time, Anne was a voracious reader, and Miep and Mr. Koophuis made sure there was a steady supply of books for her. She was fond of Greek mythology and also tackled difficult German writers, such as Goethe and Schiller. Her hobby was creating family trees of Europe's royal families. More than anything else, though, Anne wrote. The others teased her for it. They would ask how she was finding so much to write about when so little was happening in the Annex. But Anne kept at it with the utmost seriousness and sense of purpose. To protect her privacy, she placed the diary and her other papers in her father's briefcase, which was kept in his room.

In her diary, Anne once described a typical day in the Secret Annex. She began at nine in the evening, with the bustle of bedtime preparations. Furniture had to be moved about as beds were unfolded and made up. Almost nothing remained where it had been during the day. The little divan on which Anne slept had to be lengthened by placing a chair at one end. Blackout curtains were put up at 10 o'clock so that the building could not be seen by German bombers, and quiet soon descended on the Annex.

At about 11:30 P.M., Mr. Dussell would return from Mr. Kraler's office downstairs, where he had gone to work or simply for some privacy. During the night, Anne usually had to use the chamber pot she kept beneath her bed. Then she would lie awake, listening to the sounds of the night. First she would check for burglars downstairs. Then she became aware of the various sleep noises of the eight Jews; to her dismay, Mr. Dussell had a repertoire of strange, loud breathing sounds that Anne found fairly unpleasant. But this was nothing compared to the chill she felt at another frequent sound—that of gunfire in the streets.

An alarm clock woke the household at 6:45 A.M.. Quickly, everyone performed his or her morning toilet; this had to be done before Opekta employees arrived for work so that the noise of running water would not be heard. Upon her arrival at the office, Miep would visit briefly to see what groceries or supplies were needed for the day. She had an unspoken agreement with a local greengrocer whereby he would discreetly overlook the oddity of her bulk purchases and set aside extra vegetables. Before going into hiding, Mr. Van Daan had made a comparable arrangement with a butcher, with whom Miep now shopped. Mr. Koophuis had a similarly compliant friend who owned a number of bakeries. Henk, meanwhile, had obtained forged ration tickets through the Dutch underground as a further strategy for securing enough food.

However, as the war progressed, food shortages became more acute, and Miep had to do a lot more scavenging to get what she needed. Even then, the food was frequently of inferior quality and from time to time made the Jews sick. The main food treat of the week, Anne reported, was a slice of liver sausage and jam on dry bread.

The hours following breakfast were taken up with lessons and reading. At lunchtime the Jews gathered in the upstairs room for soup. They were frequently joined by a visiting Elli Vossens or by Mr. Koophuis or Mr. Kraler seeking business advice from Mr. Frank or Mr. Van Daan. Naps were the order of business after lunch. Henk would visit around five o'clock and sit with the men and discuss recent news. Anne always peppered Henk with lots of questions and often sat with the men during this time. Elli showed up around half past five to inform the Jews that they were now "free"—that is, the downstairs employees had gone home. Soon it was time for Anne to help with dinner—peeling potatoes, cooking, scrubbing pots, and tidying up. Not long after this, blackout curtains were put in place, and the cycle would begin anew.

Both prison and sanctuary, the Secret Annex provided comfort but was a constant reminder of pain. The cruel truth of anti-Semitism had hounded a group of Jews out of their homes and forced them to pretend they did not exist. The life they created for themselves "inside" stood in sorry contrast to what they had known in the days before Hitler. But the ability to do even this little was what kept them from growing completely dispirited. For they knew that their fellow Jews were suffering unspeakably worse. They knew that the Germans continued to go from house to house, searching for Jews. From that they were safe, at least for the time being.

Though only 13, Anne fully comprehended this maddening paradox. As she wrote, in a remarkably accurate vision of what was going on outside the Secret Annex:

> In the evenings when it's dark, I often see rows of good, innocent people accompanied by crying children, walking on and on . . . bullied and knocked about until they almost drop. No one is spared—old people, babies, expectant mothers, the sick—each and all join in the march of death.

How fortunate we are here, so well cared for and undisturbed. We wouldn't have to worry about all this misery
were it not that we are so anxious about all those dear to
us whom we can no longer help.

I feel wicked sleeping in a warm bed, while my dearest
friends have been knocked down or have fallen into a gutter somewhere out in the cold night. I get frightened when
I think of close friends who have now been delivered into
the hands of the cruelest brutes that walk the earth. And
all because they are Jews!

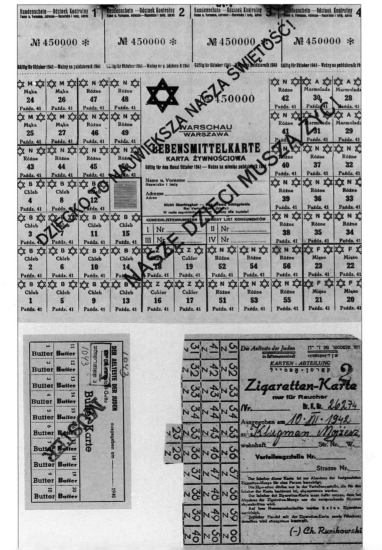

These ration tickets, in Polish (top) and German, were issued in 1941. With the tickets people could purchase flour, eggs, meat, bread, and other foodstuffs.

This photograph of Anne was taken when she was 13. Miep Gies remembered that Anne was deeply affected by the harsh realities of being a Jew in the occupied Netherlands: "On the outside, Anne was a delicate, vivacious . . . girl, but on the inside, a part of her was suddenly much older."

5

Close Quarters—
The Years Inside

LIFE IN THE SECRET ANNEX was nothing if not an exercise in compromise. With space, food, and privacy at a premium, flexibility was the key to achieving some semblance of "ordinary" life. Everyone had to be willing to adapt to the demands of these new, straitened circumstances.

The backdrop of fear made everything that much more difficult. The Jews knew that their presence might be discovered at any moment; their lives went on just a hairbreadth away from deportation and death. Tempers ran hotter than usual, and mood swings from hope to despair and back again in the space of an afternoon were not uncommon. On many occasions, Anne wrote in her diary of the intense rage she felt at one thing or another, a feeling no doubt shared by the others.

Among Anne's earliest dilemmas was reconciling herself to the presence of Mrs. Van Daan. A forward, somewhat dominating woman,

Albert Dussell, Miep Gies's dentist, shared a room with Anne Frank. Anne found Mr. Dussell bossy and referred to him in her diary as "His Lordship."

Mrs. Van Daan quickly alienated Anne with what the younger girl saw as petty behavior. For one thing, Mrs. Van Daan was upset that her dinner service, and not Mrs. Frank's, was being used, fearing its eventual decimation. Anne had not endeared herself to Mrs. Van Daan on this count, accidentally shattering one of the soup bowls. Still, Anne felt there were certainly more important things to worry about. She also hated the way Mr. and Mrs. Van Daan argued loudly in front of everyone and the tone in their voices when they did so. The Frank household had been free of such overt animosity.

Mrs. Van Daan had also withdrawn her sheets from the common linen closet and opined that children should not read books written for adults. This last opinion was particularly galling to Anne, who had become dedicated to reading and learning. Worse, Mrs. Van Daan had the maddening habit of prefacing her comments on Anne's behavior with a phrase that implied criticism of her upbringing and thus of Mrs. Frank: "If Anne were my daughter . . ." Anne's verdict on her new housemate: "Unbearable."

Peter Van Daan struck Anne early on as an unformed and uninteresting adolescent. However, beginning in 1944, Anne's opinions about Peter changed; she reached out to him for companionship, and they became good friends.

Mr. Dussell she found imperious and dubbed him "His Lordship." Dussell regarded Anne's work as trifling and was reluctant to share the table in their bedroom, which Anne wanted to use as a desk for just a few hours per week. He also joined in the general critique of Anne's behavior and had another annoying habit: He hogged the bathroom. Anne's verdict on her roommate: "A stodgy, old-fashioned disciplinarian, and preacher of long-drawn-out sermons on manners."

Anne had much more respect for her older sister. She did not seem to mind that Margot benefited from what she saw as slightly preferred treatment on the part of her parents. Nor was Anne jealous of what she viewed as Margot's more compelling beauty. They were sisters, and there was an automatic bond regardless of these differences.

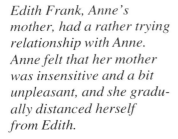

Edith Frank, Anne's mother, had a rather trying relationship with Anne. Anne felt that her mother was insensitive and a bit unpleasant, and she gradually distanced herself from Edith.

The other adolescent in the Annex was Peter Van Daan, who struck Anne early on as exceedingly unformed and uninteresting. "What a fool!" she wrote.

Whatever disdain Anne felt for the non-family members in the Annex was more than compensated for by the adoration she felt for her father. Otto Frank was a mostly towering figure for Anne—a successful businessman, a good Jew who had had the foresight to prepare a hiding place for his family, and the unquestioned arbiter of disputes in the Secret Annex. Anne looked up to him, sought him out for advice, and trusted him to keep her writings safely hidden in his briefcase. She set for herself the goal of winning his love—not just as a father loves his child but for her, Anne, as a person.

The strength of Anne's feelings for her father was a stark contrast to the emotional chasm that separated her and her mother. In Anne's view, Edith Frank lacked the sensitivity and sweetness required of a good mother. Anne remembered with pain the day her mother commented, almost casually, that she considered her daughters more like friends than daughters. Anne thought a mother owed her children more than that and gradually distanced herself. At one point she confessed to her diary, "I have to be my own mother. . . . I am my own skipper and later on I shall see where I come to land."

Were these clashes the inevitable result of close quarters and horrible circumstances inside and outside the Secret Annex? Would any group of eight people forced to live like this erupt in similar ways? Or was it an unfortunate collison of personalities that just did not get along?

As she pondered these questions, Anne managed to find some amusement in the general discord. As she wrote, "I've learned one thing now. You only really get to know people when you've had a jolly good row with them. Then and then only can you judge their true characters!" Mostly, though, she contemplated her new life in the Annex and did so with increasing acuity.

For a young girl, Anne possessed an uncommon degree of self-awareness—enough to recognize her own contribution to the fray. She knew she was a chatterbox; she enjoyed talking to people and was not at all shy about startling or provoking them by voicing the truth. She was impulsive, given to nervous outbursts that annoyed the others. She was sensitive to slights, but this was a recent phenomenon because so many seemed to be aimed in her direction. Why, she wondered, was she being singled out? Certainly, she told herself, she could not be as bad as the others made her out to be.

As she stewed and analyzed the goings-on in the Annex, she arrived at some clear views as to how things should be done and about what was right and what was wrong. Those views, indeed her entire way of thinking, came into sharper focus as the months wore on and she matured.

The autumn of 1942 brought news of enormous round-ups of Jews for deportation. Anne cried at hearing of friends and neighbors who had been herded together at Amsterdam's central railroad station and forced onto special trains. The BBC started to report that Jews were being gassed in concentration camps in Poland.

That year's Jewish Festival of Lights, Hanukkah—an eight-day celebration that commemorates the victory of the Maccabees over the Syrians in 165 B.C. and the rededication of the Temple of Jerusalem, which culminated in a religiously significant lighting of lights—was celebrated in a somewhat dimmer fashion than usual. Because of a candle shortage in the Annex, the holiday lights were allowed to burn for only 10 minutes. St. Nicholas Day, a non-Jewish holiday falling around the same time of year, was more festive. Everyone was given a small present—Anne received a doll—and traditional rhyming poems were recited. Not long after the New Year, on February 2, 1943, news of the German surrender at the Battle of Stalingrad sparked hopes that the war had turned decisively in the Allies' favor.

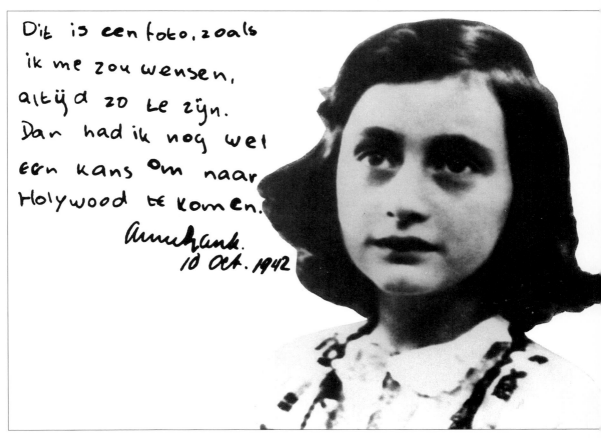

Dit is een foto, zoals ik me zou wensen, altijd zo te zijn. Dan had ik nog wel een kans om naar Holywood te komen.

Annefrank.
10 Oct. 1942

Miep Gies remembers the winter of 1942–43 changing the mood upstairs. As she wrote, "I became aware of a kind of flagging of energy up in the Annex. . . . It was as though some of the spirit had gone out of the people upstairs, and a kind of languor had taken over." Miep could see it in their faces as well—the lack of fresh air and vitamins had given Anne and the others a pale and pasty complexion.

Though the Battle of Stalingrad proved to be a turning point in the war, the conflict immediately overhead continued unabated. The Annex often shook from the roar of planes and from the bombing of Amsterdam itself. The air was filled with the smell of smoke and fire, and in the evening the sound of gunfire punctuated any attempts at

In the margin of her diary, on October 10, 1942, Anne wrote: "This is a photo as I would wish myself to look all the time. Then I would maybe have a chance to come to Hollywood."

sleep. If the house they were hiding in were hit by bombs, they would be discovered, or worse, be killed. Anne was frequently so scared she sought refuge in her father's bed, all the while knowing it was childish of her but feeling more secure for having done so.

The house continued to thunder as well from arguments between its residents. On one occasion, Edith Frank told Mr. Van Daan, "I can't bear your stupid chatter any longer." Anne's relationship with her mother reached a low point when Anne refused to allow her, in place of her

Anne thought that this 1939 photo of her father was his nicest photograph. Anne looked up to her father and frequently asked him for advice.

father, to join her for her bedtime prayers. Stung, a tearful Mrs. Frank told Anne, "I don't want to be cross, love cannot be forced." Otto Frank's reproachful looks told Anne what he thought of her behavior, but she was un-apologetic.

In the spring of 1943 the Jews confronted one of their greatest fears—a medical emergency. They had worried ever since they went into hiding that someone might fall ill; the chances of finding a doctor to treat a Jew were virtually nonexistent. But Anne had begun to complain of headaches and was having problems with her eyes. The amateur diagnosis settled on a relatively low-level condition: because of her squinting and straining to read in near-dark conditions, Anne had grown to need glasses. Miep knew of a nearby eye doctor and wanted to take Anne there on bicycle. But Anne was petrified at the idea of venturing outside and thought she might faint at her first step. Finally it was decided that she would have to wait until after the war to get glasses. Still, the Jews had had a scare. What if the next complaint was more serious?

Tensions were not so high in the household that birthdays were not acknowledged. On June 12, 1943, Anne's 14th birthday, her father presented her with a long poem he had written, which read in part:

> Correction sometimes take against your will,
> Though it's like swallowing a bitter pill,
> Which must be done if we're to keep the peace,
> While time goes by till all this suffering cease.
> You read and study nearly all the day,
> Who might have lived a different way.
> You're never bored and bring us all fresh air.
> Your only moan is this: 'What can I wear?'

Anne was tickled by her father's effort. Otto Frank had again shown himself in his best light, clearly sensitive to his daughter's growing pains—psychological and physical. Anne was indeed bursting out of her clothing, as would any adolescent experiencing a growth spurt. But this did not stop her from donning sweaters and skirts from time to time, trying to decide what she might wear back to school if the war ended and classes resumed in September or October. She was hoping not to miss a second year of school and had been cheered by the downfall of the Italian Fascist Benito Mussolini and the capitulation of Italy in September.

But the war dragged on, and with it more bad news arrived in the Annex. Miep told them that there were hardly any Jews left in Amsterdam and that often Jews were found floating in the canals—most likely those who had died while in hiding. How else could the Jews' former protectors quickly dispose of the bodies without getting caught themselves? As the prospect of a second winter in captivity made itself apparent, gloom settled on the Secret Annex. Meals began to be taken in silence.

Anne became more and more withdrawn, pursuing her studies and reading to take her mind off the arguments within and the situation outside. She yearned to find someone to talk to and confide in—about her feelings, ideals, and all the other things she had been thinking about for so long. She was not simply the incessant chatterer most of the Annex assumed she was.

There was another, more profound side to her that they had hardly seen—or misunderstood if they did. For the most part, Anne had kept this side of her personality to herself. How, she wondered, could she find a way to express the things she felt? How much longer would she have to go on feeling stifled?

Tears came much more often now—when alone in her room or down in the private office to which she would sometimes escape. In her desperation, she wrote in late October 1943 of feeling "like a songbird whose wings have been clipped and who is hurling himself in utter darkness against the bars of his cage." She dearly wanted a girlfriend, and the longing pained her incessantly.

It was around this time that Anne began to have powerful, vivid thoughts and dreams of Lies Goosens. Lies had been taken away by the Nazis in June 1943; it is unclear whether or not Anne was aware of this. But her imagination conjured up a vision of Lies, thin and drawn and dressed in rags, that was a hauntingly realistic approximation of current conditions in the concentration camp. "Oh, Anne," Lies's apparition seemed to be saying, "why have you deserted me? Help, oh, help me, rescue me from this hell!"

Anne was distressed at her helplessness and angry at the distance that now separated her from Lies. Anne had been spared, at least for the time being, and remained safe while her friend had been condemned to die. Prior to the war, Anne reasoned, there had been no difference between them when it came to virtue. Why had fate treated them so disparately? Anne prayed that God would protect her friend and wrote that Lies "seems to be a symbol to me of the sufferings of all my girl friends and all Jews. When I pray for her, I pray for all Jews and all those in need."

In December 1943, another St. Nicholas Day came and went, more subdued than the last. Anne and her father perked up spirits with rhyming poems they had composed for everyone. On New Year's Eve, Miep arrived bearing a cake on which she had iced a simple message: "Peace 1944!"

In the first days of the new year, Anne took a bold step toward solving her longing for someone to talk to: She made overtures of companionship to Peter Van Daan. Anne realized that she had underestimated Peter. He was actually a handsome, shy young man with a retiring manner that Anne had mistaken for smugness. Having dismissed him once, she was now determined to reach him and communicate with him.

Anne wrote in her diary that if the Van Daans had had a daughter, she would have sought her out just the same; the point, pure and simple, was that she needed a friend. But as her friendship with Peter developed over the following weeks, Anne became increasingly enamored of Peter, even though she was uncertain of his feelings for her. Was she a nuisance? Or was he, too, in need of a confidant? Did he share the others' view of Anne as an incurable chatterbox? Or could he see beyond that outer nervousness to the more thoughtful young woman who was searching for a soul mate?

These were among the thoughts that ran through Anne's mind as she and Peter talked and exchanged lingering gazes into each other's eyes. Evenings after dinner became their favorite time together. In the dim light of the attic, they would talk and peer out the window, hoping for a glimpse of the moon. Slowly but surely, the relationship adopted all the signs of a budding romance.

But it was not until a Saturday night in March that Anne felt that she and Peter had truly experienced a meeting of the minds. A brave Anne broke the ice, telling Peter how she felt about all the quarrels in the Annex and about her parents. She confided that she often cried her heart out in frustration over her loneliness and the state of her life in the Annex. A sensitive Peter responded in kind, speaking of his family and feelings of inadequacy. He admitted that he, too, often felt frustrated and that he responded with silence and by retreating to the attic and swearing to himself in rage.

The two young people compared notes about how they had changed in their nearly two years in hiding, and they even shared their initial opinions of each other. Anne learned that at first blush Peter considered her talkative and unruly. Anne observed that her chattering and his silences were not really very different—they were both inarticulate responses to a difficult situation. Each of them, they realized, had inner needs that were not being fulfilled in the course of daily life in the Annex.

Anne was so thrilled at this breakthrough that she called the experience the "most wonderful evening I have ever had in the 'Secret Annex.'" She soon told her diary that

Peter had fallen in love with her, but as for her own feelings, it was too early to tell. She and Peter began to sit close together when they talked, gingerly placing their arms around each other or tentatively resting their heads on each other's shoulders. In April, Anne devoted an entire diary entry to an excited account of her first kiss, noting that at 15 she was "starting very soon." "Oh, Anne, how scandalous!" she wrote. She also wondered whether her parents would approve if they knew.

Otto and Edith Frank had indeed noticed their daughter's new attachment; hardly anything in the Annex went unremarked. Anne's nightly descents from the attic usually prompted questions from parents on both sides of the relationship: Where have you been all this time? What have you been doing?

General Dwight D. Eisenhower speaks to Allied paratroopers in England on June 6, 1944, shortly before they are to board their planes to begin the invasion of Normandy.

Edith Frank was worried that her daughter was being a pest and forbade her to go upstairs, saying that Mrs. Van Daan was jealous. Otto Frank did not think that this was a problem but did caution Anne that in a confined space there could be terrible problems if things went wrong. An increasingly independent Anne bristled at the interference of her parents; why, she asked, could not love be allowed to blossom if that was what was going to happen?

Eventually, the passions between Anne and Peter subsided, and they settled into a comfortably close friendship. Though she still longed to spend time with him, by June Anne had also come to sense some of Peter's limitations. He was still, despite all their talk, a remote young man who kept most of his innermost feelings to himself. She also disliked Peter's disdain for religion, thinking it a failure of will. The thought crossed her mind that perhaps her feelings for him had been exaggerated—by youth, by her need to connect with another person, and by the unique stresses of the Annex.

Anne's perspective on her relationship with Peter also may have been the product of the new sense of purpose that had come to her of late. In late March she heard a Radio Orange broadcast saying that ordinary documents such as letters, postcards, and diaries were needed to provide the true history of what had happened in the Netherlands during the war. After the war, the broadcast said, a national center would be created to collect and publish these materials.

Anne took what she heard to heart and immediately set to work rewriting much of the diary she had been keeping, giving it more polish, and writing her text on loose sheets of paper. By this time, too, she had become a better writer, a fact she herself had recognized. Though thoughts of being a writer or journalist may have occurred to her previously, from this point on Anne was certain of her vocation. As she wrote, "I want to go on living even after my death! And therefore I am grateful to God for giving me this gift, this possibility of developing myself and of writing, of expressing all that is in me."

The Easter burglary disrupted life in the Annex for a few days. But Anne remained immersed in her diary. In increasingly sophisticated language and with new depth of feeling, she decried the stupidity of war, denounced the prevalence of anti-Semitism, and commiserated about society's treatment of women. She expressed a desire to see the great cities of Paris and London after the war and a determination not to lead a "narrow, cramped existence like Mummy and Margot . . . and all the women who do their work and are then forgotten. I must have something besides a husband and children, something that I can devote myself to!"

At the same time she indulged her imagination by crafting fables and short stories that were not included in the diary. Some of this work contains obvious parallels to Anne's life in the Annex. For instance, "The Porter's Family" mentions a woman who plays loud jazz music on a record player while sitting in a shower stall as a way of obscuring the sound of gunfire outside. The protagonist of "Kathy," meanwhile, is a lonely girl constantly criticized by her mother.

Other stories, however, represent further leaps of Anne's abilities as a writer. In a fairy tale, "Eve's Dream," Anne anthropomorphized flowers and trees to comment metaphorically on human nature. And in "The Wise Old Dwarf" she created a tiny forest world of elves, dwarfs, and sorcerers to tell a simple tale of how different people can come to live together by understanding one another's needs and desires.

On June 6, 1944, the long-awaited Allied invasion of Europe began. Anne listened as U.S. general Dwight D. Eisenhower spoke of achieving "complete victory" before the end of the year. General Charles de Gaulle of France, King George VI of England, and English prime minister Winston Churchill followed with moving speeches. Then, in July, came news of an unsuccessful assassination attempt against Hitler. Finally, it seemed, someone had been brave enough to try to end the madness at its source. Anne and the others felt newly imbued with strength. Could peace truly be just over the horizon?

Meanwhile, for Anne, the words continued to pour forth in a torrent. Whereas once there were several days or even weeks between diary entries, now she wrote nearly every day, and at length. She addressed the nature of faith, believing in the power of religion and of striving to uphold one's honor and conscience before the eyes of God. She wrote of her love of nature, thinking it the best way to experience the presence of God. She expressed disappointment with her father for not understanding her need to be addressed as a person in her own right and not as just another youth going through a difficult adolescence. As she did with her mother, Anne ended up keeping her father at a distance, revealing little of her true thoughts and feelings to him.

It was clear to the others in the Annex that by this time Anne's diary had become her life. Miep Gies remembered interrupting Anne at work in July 1944:

> I saw that Anne was writing intently, and hadn't heard
> me. I was quite close to her and was about to turn and go
> when she looked up, surprised, and saw me standing
> there. . . . I saw a look on her face at this moment that I'd
> never seen before. It was a look of dark concentration, as
> if she had a throbbing headache. This look pierced me,
> and I was speechless. She was suddenly another person
> there writing at the table. I couldn't say a word. My eyes
> were locked with Anne's brooding ones. . . . I was upset
> by Anne's dark mood. . . . It was as if I had interrupted an
> intimate moment in a very, very private friendship.

Miep was accurate in her reading of Anne's demeanor. For more than two years, Anne had been struggling with what it meant to come of age in an era of unspeakable horror.

The dreams, hopes, and ideals that arise naturally within any young person—the hallmarks of growth—were in Anne shattered in a most terrifying manner, squelched by her confinement and by the brutal facts of Fascist dictatorship and war. The adults in the Annex had had their youth. Anne's was spent alone, physically and spiritually, a predicament she had little hope of changing. This was the tragedy that she took most to heart and that tore at her the most.

On August 1, 1944, Anne wrote that she was a "little bundle of contradictions." On the one hand, there was the exuberant, gregarious girl that everyone knew—and criticized. On the other, there was the more sedate and thoughtful young woman within who was scared of not being taken seriously. Anne was well aware of this dual personality; she had remarked on it many times. But on this date she seemed especially troubled and exhausted by it; the burden of other people's perceptions weighed upon her. Still, she vowed to "keep on trying to find a way of becoming what I would so like to be, and what I could be, if . . . there weren't any other people living in the world."

Her efforts were cut short, for these were the last words Anne Frank recorded in her diary.

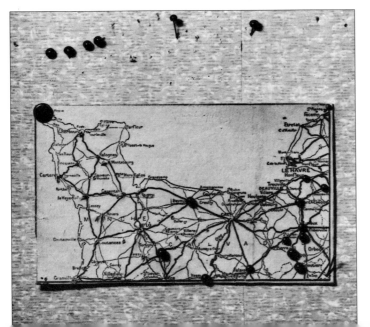

Anne and the others kept track of the progress of the Allied troops after the Normandy invasion using this map, which they tacked to a wall of the Secret Annex.

Bergen-Belsen, the German concentration camp where Anne and her sister, Margot, were finally interned, was under the direct supervision of Gestapo chief Heinrich Himmler, the mastermind of Hitler's extermination campaign.

6

The Last Seven Months

THE FIRST WEEK OF AUGUST 1944 marked two months since the Allied invasion of Normandy. Across occupied Europe, expectations were high that this great offensive would send the Germans into final retreat and end the war. Anne Frank was one month into her third year in hiding. She knew from Radio Orange that the American First Army (29th Division) had won the crucial battle for Saint-Lô, which had served as an important defense base for the Germans, and were marching toward Paris. After that, she hoped, would come Belgium and the Netherlands.

But on August 4 her dreams of freedom died when a German in uniform appeared suddenly in the doorway of the front office at 263 Prinsengracht. Brandishing a revolver and accompanied by several policemen who were not in uniform, Karl Josef Silberbauer, a member of the SS, glared at Miep Gies and said, "Stay put. Don't move." (*SS* is an abbreviation for *Schutzstaffel*, or the Nazi elite guard, which served as Hitler's bodyguard and as a police force.)

Silberbauer walked to the back office where Mr. Kraler worked. The policemen fanned out into the building's offices and corridors.

They seemed to know just where to go. A trembling Jo Koophuis turned to Miep and said, "I think the time has come."

A few minutes later, on the second-floor landing, one of the policemen ordered Mr. Kraler to open the swinging cupboard. "But there's only a bookcase there!" he protested.

The man grabbed the cupboard himself and pulled, and the secret door swung back to reveal a staircase. A gun at his back, Mr. Kraler was forced to climb to the top of the steps. There he saw Mrs. Frank standing at a table in her bedroom. Anne was with her. The other Jews were quickly rounded up, brought to this same room, searched for weapons, and told to stand with their hands up.

Silberbauer, joining the group, ordered Otto Frank to reveal where the Jews kept their valuables. Then he picked up Mr. Frank's briefcase and scattered its contents—Anne's diaries and papers—onto the floor. In their place he put the Jews' jewelry and money. Anne and the others were then allowed to pack some clothing and toiletries. A vehicle had been summoned and was on its way.

A little while later, Silberbauer addressed Miep downstairs. "Aren't you ashamed that you are helping Jewish garbage?" he said with a snarl. "You have betrayed your country, you deserve the worst." But when the transport arrived and the eight Jews, Kraler, and Koophuis were taken away to Gestapo headquarters, Miep was not among them. She had recognized Silberbauer's accent as that of someone from Vienna. She, too, was Viennese, and she told him as much. Silberbauer seemed to calm down. Apparently, this was enough to win Miep a reprieve. But Silberbauer parted with a warning: "As a personal favor, I'm going to let you stay here, but if you run away, we'll take your husband. . . . I know he's involved."

With the Nazis gone, Miep went with a workman, who had the keys, and Elli up to the Secret Annex. They had to hurry; the Nazis could return at any moment. The place had been ransacked in the search for more valuables. On the floor of what had been the Franks' bedroom Miep noticed the papers, notebooks, and diaries Anne had filled with her writings. Quickly, she and Elli gathered everything she could and put them in her desk down in the office. A few days later, Miep went upstairs again to retrieve still more of Anne's papers. "I'll keep everything safe for Anne until she comes back," she told herself and put them in a drawer. A few days later, a truck sent by the Nazi authorities came to the Secret Annex and carted off all of the Jews' remaining belongings.

As anguish filled those left behind at 263 Prinsengracht, their thoughts centered on a single question: Who had betrayed Anne and the others to the Nazis? The Jews had been careless from time to time, but after more than two years in hiding their routines could be regarded as successful. Likewise, their existence was not uncovered as part of a larger German raid on the block or neighborhood. Rather, it seemed clear from the way the Germans swooped down

People arrive at Wester-bork, the transit camp, before they are to be transported to Auschwitz, the concentration camp in Poland. By the time the Franks had arrived at Westerbork, the Germans had already transported more than 100,000 Dutch Jews to death camps.

On September 29, 1944, German prisoners under the guard of American troops march past a cheering crowd in Limbricht, the Netherlands. The Franks, Van Daans, and Mr. Dussell were among the last Jews shipped to Auschwitz before the Allies captured Brussels on September 3.

on 263 Prinsengracht and made their way right to the swinging cupboard door that they had been tipped off by an informer.

Several official inquiries have been conducted over the years, seeking to determine who it could have been. For a time, suspicion focused on one of the warehouse workmen. But the Netherlands State Institute for War Documentation concluded that although this man may have guessed cor-

rectly that there were Jews present in the building, it was impossible to reconstruct exactly what happened and name him definitively as the informer.

Silberbauer was questioned after the war but did not remember who the betrayer was. As he said in a sad comment on the occupation: "I don't remember. There were so many betrayals during those years." Postwar interrogation of another former Nazi did reveal that the informer, whoever he or she was, had received the standard reward for putting fugitive Jews into the hands of the Nazis: about $1.40 per Jew, for a total of $11.20.

The Nazis released Mr. Koophuis from detention because of a medical condition. Mr. Kraler was sent to a forced labor camp but escaped after eight months and spent the remainder of the war hiding in his own home. The Franks, Van Daans, and Mr. Dussell were taken from Gestapo headquarters to Weteringschans prison and then to Westerbork, the transit camp—*Judendurchgangslager* in German. Westerbork was the first stop for Dutch Jews on the way to Auschwitz.

Little is known of what happened to Anne Frank at Westerbork. She and her family were placed in the punishment barracks reserved for those who had been in hiding or who were members of the Dutch resistance. Janny Brandes-Brilleslijper, who had done some work for the resistance and was also in Westerbork, said after the war that she saw the Franks at Amsterdam's central railroad station on August 8, the day they were shipped to Westerbork. She remembered Anne and Margot wearing "sporty clothes, with sweatsuits and backpacks, as if they were going on a winter vacation."

By the time the Franks arrived in Westerbork, it was thought that there would not be another shipment of Dutch Jews to the death camps. More than 100,000 Dutch Jews, roughly 75 percent of the Netherlands's prewar Jewish population, had already been shipped to Auschwitz and other camps. But the Germans faced a rapidly deteriorating position on the battlefield and had begun their retreat from westernmost Europe. Indeed, on August 25, Allied forces liberated France. But on September 3, the day the Allies captured Brussels, the Germans herded 1,019 Dutch Jews—498 men, 442 women, and 79 children—onto a freight train. This would be the last shipment of Dutch Jews to leave the Netherlands, and the Franks, Van Daans, and Mr. Dussell were on it. Two days later—two days too late for Anne Frank—the Germans began their retreat from the Netherlands.

Crammed like cattle into a windowless freight car, Anne and her companions languished without food or water for three days as the train made a slow, creaking journey to Auschwitz, in Poland. If this train had been like the others that had ferried Jews to their deaths throughout the war, there would have been barely any room to sit down; only the neediest—the ill, the elderly, and pregnant women, for example—were granted a few inches of floor space so they could rest. Toilet facilities consisted of a bucket or two that quickly overflowed, filling an already stifling car with a nauseating stench. The sound of people moaning from weariness or pain was constant. The few times the doors of the car were opened, growling guard dogs made sure the Jews did not contemplate trying to escape. Their Nazi handlers would heap verbal abuse upon them. "Dirty Jew!" they would taunt. "Filth!"

The train carrying Anne Frank reached Auschwitz on the night of September 5–6, 1944. Immediately upon arrival, men and women were separated. This was the last Otto Frank saw of Edith, Margot, and Anne. Next, the Jews

At Auschwitz men and women are separated by the Nazis. After their separation men and women were stripped, tattooed with an identification number, and then either worked to death or sent to the gas chambers.

were forced to strip and were then tattooed on the arm with an identifying number. Survivors carry this scar with them permanently. Then, under the glare of bright spotlights, the Jews were led to a platform where death camp officials would make a "selection"—who would live and who would die.

Of the 1,019 Jews on the last train from Westerbork, 258 men and 212 women were deemed healthy enough to be "admitted" to Auschwitz. They would be worked nearly to death and then killed. The rest—including all children under the age of 15—were sent immediately to gas chambers that had been disguised as showers. Their bodies were then brought to the crematoria, whose blazing fires sent a hellish red glow into the sky and an unforgettable smell into the nostrils of everyone in the camp, condemned and commandant alike. It was a ruthlessly efficient operation. At Auschwitz, the biggest of the Nazi death camps, some 2 million Jews had already been gassed by the time Anne arrived. By war's end, the Nazis killed approximately 6 million Jews, 75 percent of Europe's prewar Jewish population of 8 million.

Anne and Margot were admitted to Auschwitz and assigned to one of the women's barracks, which housed thousands of prisoners. Like all the women, Anne was given a sackcloth smock as her sole piece of clothing. Her thick, dark hair, of which she was so fond and proud, was clipped to its roots, allowing the sun to burn the tender skin of her newly shaven scalp. All other body hair—including her pubic hair—was shaved as well.

The women were organized into groups of five. Anne was the leader of her group, even though she was the youngest. Among her responsibilities was dividing the hunks of black bread that formed part of the daily food ration. One camp survivor recalled that Anne "did it so well and fairly that there was none of the usual grumbling."

The daily ration of moldy gruel was not enough to keep the women alive. Most of them developed blisters and sores because of a lack of vitamins. Both Anne and Margot developed scabies, a skin rash, and spent some of their time at Auschwitz in the so-called *Krätzeblock*, or "scabies barracks." Severe stomach cramps and diarrhea were another common ailment. The latrine consisted of an open outdoor sewer, without toilet paper or privacy. Eventually, most women stopped menstruating.

The women were packed like sardines onto rickety wooden barracks beds and, if lucky, had some straw for a mattress. Lice, bedbugs, and rats were their bunkmates. If someone died, her body was brought outside and placed in front of the barracks. The women had to walk by the mounting pile on their way to the latrine.

Roll calls roused the women from bed at any time of day or night. They were expected to stand, for hours on end, sometimes in the rain and bitter cold, while the Germans counted, counted again, and then recounted their prisoners, making a seemingly endless tally of those who would soon be killed.

Electrified fences divided Auschwitz into smaller, more manageable sectors. Sometimes, to end their torment, women would commit suicide by running deliberately into these barricades. They were left to dangle where they had died as an example to the others. So were those who tried to escape but were shot in the back. Other transgressors were hanged in public, with the prisoners forced to watch.

One woman who was with Anne in Auschwitz later recalled: "I can still see [Anne] standing at the door and looking down the camp street as a herd of naked Gypsy girls was driven by to the crematory, and Anne watched them go and cried. And she cried also when we marched past the Hungarian children who had already been waiting half a day in the rain in front of the gas chambers because it was not yet their turn. And Anne nudged me and said: 'Look, look. Their eyes . . .'"

In October 1944, Anne Frank was subjected to another "selection"—this one for women who would be trans-

Anne and Margot were transferred to Bergen-Belsen in October 1944. When someone died in a concentration camp, his or her body was usually brought outside and placed in front of the barracks. People had to walk by the pile of bodies on their way to the latrine.

ferred from Auschwitz to Bergen-Belsen, in Germany. Bergen-Belsen was under the directorship of Heinrich Himmler, who was chief of the Gestapo and was in charge of the establishment of concentration camps and the internment of Jews and other people. Himmler directed Hitler's extermination campaign and was very successful as a propagandist—Bergen-Belsen was described as one of the "better" camps, if such distinctions can even be drawn. It was used to house prisoners who would be traded for Germans held by the Allies. However, conditions were deplorable, and hunger and disease were widespread. Around 50,000 Russian prisoners of war had died at Bergen-Belsen from infected water, little food, no medication, and no heat or housing. Still, if Anne was transferred to Bergen-Belsen, she stood a better chance of surviving the war.

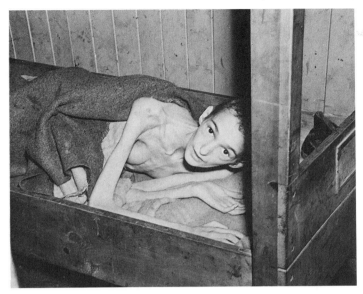

A woman suffering from malnutrition and overwork lies in bed in the barracks at Bergen-Belsen. Most barracks were infested with lice, rats, and bedbugs.

Stripped again and naked under the cruel, bright lights of the selection hall, the women submitted again to the humiliating scrutiny of the German authorities. One camp survivor remembers seeing Anne that night: "[Anne] took Margot's arm and they came forward. . . . Anne turned her serene face toward us; then they were led away. It was impossible to see what happened behind the light, and Mrs. Frank cried, 'The children! My God! My God!'"

In late October, Anne, Margot, and Mrs. Van Daan were transferred to Bergen-Belsen. On December 20, 1944, Albert Dussell died in the Neuengamme concentration camp in Germany, the second of the Secret Annex Jews to die. Edith Frank was next. Devastated by the separation from her daughters and now alone at Auschwitz, she died on January 6, 1945.

As it turned out, conditions at Bergen-Belsen were little better than those at Auschwitz. The main problems were a raging typhus epidemic and severe overcrowding. Rachel Van Amerongen-Frankfoorder, who was with Anne at Bergen-Belsen, remembers that Anne and Margot "had the least desirable places in the barracks, below, near the door, which was constantly opened and closed. You heard them constantly screaming, 'Close the door, close the door,' and the voices became weaker every day. They were the youngest among us."

Anne and Lies Goosens had a cheerless reunion at Bergen-Belsen. Lies had believed that Anne had escaped with her family to Switzerland. Anne thought that Lies had died. But the camp grapevine had helped them find each other, and there they were, in adjacent sectors, divided by an electrified fence but still able to get close enough on a few occasions to compare their desperate circumstances.

Lies later recalled the night she saw Anne again for the first time:

> I waited shivering in the darkness . . . suddenly I heard a voice. "Lies, Lies? Where are you?" It was Anne, and I ran in the direction of the voice, and then I saw her beyond the barbed wire. She was in rags. I saw her emaciated, sunken face in the darkness. Her eyes were very large. We cried and cried, for now there was only the barbed wire between us, nothing more. And no longer any difference in our fates.
>
> I told Anne that my mother had died and my father was dying, and Anne told me that she knew nothing about her father, but that her mother had stayed behind in Auschwitz. Only Margot was still with her, but she was already very sick. . . . It wasn't the same Anne. She was a broken girl. I probably was, too, but it was so terrible. She immediately began to cry, and she told me, "I don't have any parents anymore." . . . I always think if Anne had known that her father was still alive, she might have had more strength to survive.

During the last of their meetings, Lies tossed a small parcel of food over the fence. Lies last saw Anne scurrying to retrieve the package, only to be outraced by another hungry prisoner. Shortly after this, Anne was transferred to another section of the camp.

Janny Brandes-Brilleslijper recalled that at one point around this time, "Anne stood in front of me, wrapped in a blanket. She didn't have any more tears. Oh, we hadn't had tears for a long time. And she told me that she had such a horror of the lice and fleas in her clothes that she had thrown all of her clothes away. It was the middle of winter and she was wrapped in one blanket."

At the end of February or in early March 1945—the collapse of administration at the camp made it impossible to determine exactly when—Margot succumbed to the typhus epidemic and lapsed into a coma. Several days later, she was found dead on the floor of her barracks, having fallen from her bunk. Anne, meanwhile, was also sick with typhus—so sick that she was never told of Margot's death. A camp survivor said later that "after a few days Anne sensed [Margot's death], and soon afterwards she died, peacefully, feeling that nothing bad was happening to her." The two girls' bodies were thrown into a mass grave. On

Lies Goosens, Anne Frank's friend, survived Bergen-Belsen. Years later, Lies recalled her cheerless reunion with Anne at the camp and their horrible treatment by the Nazis.

April 15, 1945, Bergen-Belsen was liberated by the British.

By this time, the advance of the Soviet Red Army had led the Nazis to abandon Auschwitz and to retreat toward Germany. The Nazis set about destroying the crematoria and any other evidence of the mass murders they had committed and took many of their prisoners on what they called "evacuation expeditions" but were more aptly known as "death marches." The weakened prisoners were in no state to keep up with the pace, and many simply died en route. Others were shot and left by the side of the road. Peter Van Daan left Auschwitz on one of these death marches and was never heard from again. According to the Red Cross, he survived the march but died on May 5, 1945, in the Mauthausen concentration camp in Austria, three days before it was liberated. His mother, Petronella Van Daan, was transferred from camp to camp and died, according to the Red Cross, "between April 9 and May 8, 1945, in Germany or in Czechoslovakia." According to the Netherlands State Institute for War Documentation's *Diary of Anne Frank: The Critical Edition* (1989), Hermann Van Daan was immediately sent to the gas chambers upon his arrival at Auschwitz. However, Otto Frank

British troops liberated Bergen-Belsen on April 15, 1945. Shortly after they arrived, the British had to burn down the camp because of a typhus epidemic.

reported meeting Van Daan at Auschwitz sometime later. Frank said that sometime in October or November 1944, Van Daan had hurt his thumb while working at the camp and had asked to go back to the barracks. It just so happened that on that particular day the Nazis did not have enough people to meet their quota in the gas chambers and had gone to the barracks to round up more. Van Daan was among those who were taken to be gassed.

On April 30, 1945, Adolf Hitler committed suicide in his Berlin air-raid shelter. Within days, Germany surrendered unconditionally, and the war in Europe was over.

That left Otto Frank as the only one of the Jews from the Secret Annex to survive the war. He was in Auschwitz when it was liberated by the Russians. From there he went by train to Odessa, a Ukrainian port on the Black Sea, and then journeyed by ship to Marseilles, on the southern coast of France. He arrived back in Amsterdam on June 3, 1945. He had heard that his wife had died and that his daughters had been sent to Bergen-Belsen. But as he told Miep upon seeing her again, "I have great hope for Margot and Anne."

Otto Frank moved in with Henk and Miep and resumed his position as head of the food-products business. Anne's birthdate—June 12—came and went with no information. One day at the end of July or in early August, while at work, he received a letter from a nurse in Rotterdam telling him of his daughters' deaths. He turned to Miep and told her the news: "Miep, Margot and Anne are not coming back."

Otto Frank went to his private office to be alone. Miep reached into her desk drawer and pulled out Anne's diaries, notebooks, and loose papers. They had not been touched since she had gathered them from the floor of the hiding place after the betrayal. Miep brought the papers to Mr. Frank, saying, "Here is your daughter's legacy." A short time later, the phone on Miep's desk rang. "Miep," said Mr. Frank. "Please see to it that I'm not disturbed." It was not the reunion Mr. Frank had been hoping for. But part of Anne had survived the war.

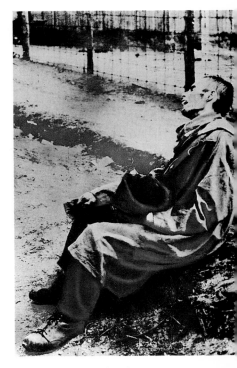

This photograph of a survivor of Bergen-Belsen was taken when the British liberated the camp. Anne and Margot both died from typhus about a month or two before the British arrived.

Anne Frank wrote toward the end of her extraordinary diary: "It's really a wonder that I haven't dropped all of my ideals, because they seem so absurd and impossible to carry out. Yet I keep them, because in spite of everything I still believe that people are really good at heart."

7

The Eternal Spirit of a Young Dutch Jew

OTTO FRANK KNEW HIS DAUGHTER had created a powerful document. But at first he gave little thought to publishing the diary as a book. Instead, he wanted certain friends and acquaintances to read the "essential" parts of Anne's writings—those entries that spoke most directly to the experiences of the war just past.

To that end he made several typescript copies of a manuscript that was based on his selections from the diaries, notebooks, and loose papers Anne had left behind. He omitted certain passages about Anne's awakening sexuality and about her clashes with her mother, thinking these private and of little interest to others.

Actually, Anne wrote two versions of her diary—the original and the one she rewrote in 1944 after hearing the radio address. The manuscript as collated by Otto Frank after the war constitutes a third version—material from Anne's two versions plus some of the writing she had done on loose sheets of paper. For his version, Otto Frank had taken more of Anne's writing from the second version of her diary.

Anne's original diary, the one that she received as a birthday present when she turned 13. Anne wrote two versions of her diary, and Otto Frank compiled a third version by combining parts of the diaries with writing Anne had done on loose sheets of paper.

Frank himself spent hours reading his daughter's writing and was profoundly moved. He was startled at the depth of her thinking and ideals and marveled at her inner courage, so rare in someone so young. All of this, however, was a side of his daughter he had rarely seen while she was alive; Anne had kept it to herself through most of her time in the Secret Annex. As a result, Otto Frank concluded, sadly, that he had never really known his daughter and that "most parents don't really know their children."

In adjusting to postwar life, Otto Frank began again to host weekly gatherings of friends for coffee and conversation. These get-togethers were much like those that had filled the Franks' apartment before the war, with one crucial difference: The war had killed most of those earlier guests. Those who joined him now were mostly Jews who had somehow, miraculously, survived the Holocaust.

On one occasion, Otto Frank mentioned Anne's diary to an acquaintance, Dr. Werner Cahn, and gave him part of it to read. Cahn was deeply impressed and tried to find a publisher for the work through his contacts in the Dutch publishing world. However, he was turned down by a

Dutch publisher and by a German publisher; there are indications that two other publishers also rejected the book.

Frank was not upset by these actions. He remained reluctant to publish, fearing an invasion of privacy for those mentioned in the diaries. But a widening circle of people who had seen the diary believed in its importance and were astonished at the publishers' indifference.

Cahn then cajoled Frank into granting him permission to show the material to a friend—Dr. Jan Romein, a prominent Dutch historian. Romein wrote an article about it that appeared in *Het Parool*, a Dutch newspaper, on April 3, 1946, and said, in part:

> If all the signs do not deceive me, this girl would have become a talented writer had she remained alive. [She] showed an insight into the failings of human nature—her own not excepted—so infallible that it would have astonished one in an adult, let alone in a child. At the same time she also highlighted the infinite possibilities of human nature, reflected in humor, tenderness and love. . . . That this girl could have been abducted and murdered proves to me that we have lost the fight against human bestiality.

The article was widely discussed and garnered much attention, including, finally, that of a Dutch publisher. Romein urged Frank to reconsider his opposition to formally publishing the diary. Frank was eventually won over by the argument that it was his duty to history, and to the Jews, to make Anne's account public. The world should learn from and never forget what had happened to the Jews, it was said, for the same thing could happen to others. The fact that Anne had retained her belief in human decency despite the evil around her was seen as another important ingredient of the diary's message.

A little more than a year later, in June 1947, *Het Achterhuis* (Dutch for *The Secret Annex*) was published in a limited edition by Contact Publishers of Amsterdam. Before long the book had gone through several editions and received virtually unanimous praise. In 1950, the book was published in Germany and France, and in 1952 it was translated into English and appeared in England and the United States as *Anne Frank: The Diary of a Young Girl*. The U.S. version, published with an introduction by Eleanor Roosevelt, wife of the late President Franklin D. Roosevelt, received widespread acclaim.

The book went on to be read throughout the world. It has been translated into more than 55 languages and has

In 1947, Contact Publishers of Amsterdam published Het Achterhuis *(The Secret Annex). The book became a best-seller, and in 1952 it was translated into English as* Anne Frank: The Diary of a Young Girl.

sold more than 20 million copies. Another volume of Anne's work, *Tales from the Secret Annex*, containing short stories, essays, and reminiscences that were not part of the diary, was published in later years. Posthumously, Anne Frank achieved her goal of becoming a famous writer.

Anne Frank: The Diary of a Young Girl touched people of all nationalities, races, and religions, but it resounded, and continues to resound, most dramatically with young people. As one 16-year-old West German girl wrote to Otto Frank: "I was in search of a friend, and now I have found her. Her name is Anne Frank." A 14-year-old American sent a letter reading in part: "Adolescents like Anne and myself must lead the way for adults—adults who can find no beauty in their world of war and hate. For we are ahead—we are not children anymore, but not yet adults, and through our childish wisdom we will try to show the world the everlasting path of harmony and peace."

Perhaps the most poignant letters came from those in the shattered countries of Germany and Japan, the aggressors of World War II. Typical was this sentiment expressed by a 22-year-old German girl:

> Often I find it hard to grasp that all is going on as before, that things are once more following their customary pattern under the pleasant cloak of the so-called high standard of living. . . . Mr. Frank, please believe that there are young people who are fully aware of the deep guilt that overwhelms the German people. My friends and I want to act in such a way that every moment bears testimony to our feelings of responsibility.

Otto Frank answered most of these letters personally and continued to do so for the rest of his life. As the diary's renown spread, he eventually retired from the food-products business to devote himself to the growing phenomenon. In the fall of 1952 he moved out of Miep and Henk's apartment to Basel, Switzerland, to be near his mother. In November 1953, he returned to Amsterdam to marry Elfriede ("Fritzi") Geiringer-Markovits, another concentration camp survivor who had lost most of her family. Together with Fritzi's daughter, Eva, they returned to Switzerland.

In 1955, the diary was also made into a highly successful play, but considerable controversy swirled around its authorship and presentation. Meyer Levin, a prominent American novelist and journalist who had witnessed the liberation of Auschwitz and other camps, became one of the book's early champions and helped find a publisher for it in the United States. In return, Otto Frank granted Levin the first chance to write a play based on the diary.

However, Levin's script was rejected by a series of producers, and the opportunity to create a suitable dramatic treatment passed to a pair of screenwriters for the Metro-Goldwyn-Mayer film studio, Albert Hackett and his wife, Frances Goodrich. Their version premiered in New York in October 1955 and was an enormous box-office success, eventually winning a Tony Award and that year's Pulitzer Prize for drama.

The play was presented in Europe the following year. The premiere performance in the Netherlands on November 27, 1956, was attended by Queen Juliana (who was the daughter of Wilhelmina and who ascended the throne in 1948). The German version opened on October 1, 1956, and was staged simultaneously in Constance, Dresden, Düsseldorf, Hamburg, Karlsruhe, West Berlin, Vienna, and Zurich. In Germany, the play met with a different kind of success: stunned silence. Often there was not even any applause. As one critic wrote:

> When the play opened . . . no one knew how the audiences would react. . . . No Nazis were seen on the stage, but their ominous presence made itself felt every minute. Finally, at the end, Nazi jackboots were heard storming

upstairs to raid the hiding place. At the end of the epilogue only Anne's father was on the stage, a lonely old man. . . . Packed audiences received Anne Frank's tragedy in a silence heavy with remorse. In Düsseldorf, people did not even go out during the intermission. They sat in their seats as if afraid of the lights outside, shamed to face each other.

Levin watched with growing anger as the play succeeded. He felt that he had been victimized by the people who had rejected his script and claimed that the Hacketts had appropriated some of his material in crafting their award-winning script. Levin brought suit against Otto Frank for fraud and breach of contract and against the Hacketts for plagiarism. Thus began a battle that consumed Levin for the rest of his life.

The 1955 production of The Diary of Anne Frank *(the Frances Goodrich and Albert Hackett dramatization of Anne Frank's diary) included the actors David Levin, Susan Strasberg, Eva Rubinstein, Joseph Schildkraut, and Lou Jacobi. The play eventually won a Tony Award and a Pulitzer Prize for drama.*

On February 24, 1967, three former Nazis convicted of sending Anne Frank and 83,000 other Jews to their deaths during World War II are sentenced to prison terms in Munich, Germany.

A jury ruled in his favor on the charge of plagiarism, but appeals dragged on for a few years. In 1959, Levin ceded his rights to the play in exchange for a payment of $15,000, which covered his legal expenses. At this point, both sides thought the dispute was over. But Levin reopened the issue in 1966 by staging his version of the play in Tel Aviv, Israel; performances were ended at the insistence of Otto Frank's lawyers.

Levin addressed the issue again in 1973 with his aptly titled book, *The Obsession*. Levin claimed that his script had been rejected because of a German-Jewish conspiracy against him, an Eastern European Jew. Among those who had read and passed judgment on the script was the writer Lillian Hellman, with whom Levin often feuded. But Hellman herself was no stranger to conspiracy, having been a victim of blacklisting during the McCarthy era of the 1950s; Levin's charges were thus seen to ring rather hollow.

Levin also objected to what he saw as the Hacketts' dilution of the diary's Jewish content. Otto Frank is known to have wanted the play to communicate a universal message to audiences and for the play to be accessible to non-Jews. Thus, certain Jewish references were edited out of the stage version. This infuriated Levin, whose version of the play had been much more explicit about anti-Semitism and Jewish identity.

Scholars who have examined the two scripts differ as to whether plagiarism occurred, though there are some startling similarities in both dialogue and the overall conception of the play. Others have asked why Otto Frank could not have permitted a second version of the play to be staged. Levin's obsession, which had earned him much ill will over the years, ended with his death in 1981.

Levin's name figured in another controversy surrounding the publication of the diary. In 1957, a Danish literary critic claimed that Levin, and not Anne Frank, was the author of the diary. This was the first salvo fired by neo-Nazis (a group espousing the programs and policies of Hitler's Nazis) and other right-wing extremists in their campaign to question the authenticity of the diary.

Unfortunately, the crushing defeat of Hitler and the Germans did not put an end to anti-Semitism or even to the hateful Nazi movement. In 1958, a German critic wrote a theater review of an adaptation of *The Adventures of Tom Sawyer* that contained this passage: "The forged diaries of Eva Braun [Hitler's mistress], of the Queen of England and the hardly more authentic one of Anne Frank may have earned several millions for the profiteers from Germany's defeat, but they have also raised our own hackles quite a bit."

Otto Frank brought suit against the author of the review and against another individual who had come to the reviewer's defense. A subsequent investigation confirmed the authenticity of the diary, but the case dissolved amid legal and procedural wrangling and was settled out of court. Otto Frank came to regret this move. As he said, "Had I but known that there would be people who would consider a settlement in this case as insufficient proof, I should certainly not have dropped the case."

Indeed, the allegations continued to be heard over the ensuing years, in Europe and the United States. So-called revisionist historians claimed the Holocaust was a hoax as well. Barely veiling their anti-Semitic, neo-Nazi sentiments, they stated, despite all the evidence to the contrary, that the gas chambers and concentration camps had never existed, that persecution of the Jews was a myth, and that the whole story was some kind of fantasy created by the Jews themselves.

In 1959, Otto Frank speaks with schoolchildren in Düsseldorf, Germany, during a cornerstone-laying ceremony for the Anne Frank School. Over the years there have been schools in the Netherlands, France, Hungary, and Brazil named in Anne's honor.

In June 17, 1957, in Frankfurt, Germany, residents watch the unveiling of the bronze plaque commemorating the home of Anne's family.

An article in the *American Mercury* stated, "Here, then, is just one more fraud in a whole series of frauds in support of the 'Holocaust' legend and the saga of the Six Million." A German publisher distributed a book called *Anne Frank's Diary—The Big Fraud*, which said, among other things, "Millions of schoolchildren have been forced and are still being forced to read this fake . . . and now it turns out that it is the product of a New York scriptwriter in collaboration with the girl's father!"

Otto Frank won a court injunction against this publisher, preventing him from distributing his lie-filled pamphlets. But the controversy continued into the 1980s. Finally, the Netherlands State Forensic Science Laboratory, working for the Netherlands State Institute for War Documentation, conducted a detailed examination of Anne's handwriting and of the paper, ink, and glue she used in keeping her diary. The lab's report concluded beyond all doubt that the diary was indeed hers and hers alone.

But the story does not stop there. Two German neo-Nazis attacked the Dutch research that proved the authenticity of the diary. In 1988–90, they were prosecuted for their statements, and a Hamburg court of appeals decided against them, heavily fining them. It can be said that the

On June 12, 1979, the 50th anniversary of Anne Frank's birth, Otto Frank shows Queen Juliana of the Netherlands the Secret Annex, in what is now called the Anne Frank House in Amsterdam.

court case set a precedent in Germany: if a person refutes the authenticity of *The Diary of Anne Frank*, or Otto Frank in his capacity as its editor, that person can expect to be prosecuted in the courts for his or her allegation.

People around the world who have read the diaries and been touched by Anne's experience have sought in many ways to keep her memory alive. In Israel, an Anne Frank Forest of 10,000 trees has been planted in the Forest of the Martyrs in the hills of Judea. The school Anne attended in Amsterdam has been renamed the Anne Frank School. There are also schools named for her in France, Hungary, Germany, and Rio de Janiero, Brazil. There are Anne Frank Homes for children and young people in Germany and Israel and an Anne Frank Village in the Netherlands started by a Nobel Peace Prize winner. The Russian poet Yevgeny Yevtushenko mentioned her in his poem "Babi Yar," which commemorates a massacre of Jews in the Ukraine during the war:

I seem to be Anne Frank
transparent
as a branch in April.

And on the family's Frankfurt home there is now a plaque reading:

In this house lived Anne Frank,
Who was born June 12, 1929 in Frankfurt am Main.
She died as a victim of the National Socialistic persecu-
tions in1945 in the concentration camp at Bergen-Belsen.
Her life and death—our responsibility.
The youth of Frankfurt.

The building at 263 Prinsengracht, now known as the Anne Frank House, has been turned into a museum. Since its official opening in May 1960, hundreds of thousands of tourists have visited the exhibits—including Anne's room, where her movie-star pictures still adorn the walls. Other visitors have taken part in educational programs run by the Anne Frank Foundation, which is dedicated to promoting harmony and creative encounters between people, especially young people of different races and nationalities.

Miep and Henk Gies stand beside the swinging cupboard, the entrance to the Secret Annex. In 1987, Miep and Henk ended nearly 40 years of silence about their assistance to Anne and the others. Miep's memoir was entitled Anne Frank Remembered: The Story of the Woman Who Helped to Hide the Frank Family.

In 1980, Otto Frank died in Switzerland at the age of 91. As of 1992, Miep and Henk Gies resided in Amsterdam. Though May 4 is the official Dutch day of mourning, another day of the calendar is, for them, just as bleak: August 4, the anniversary of the betrayal. As Miep wrote in her memoirs, "On that day . . . Henk and I stay at home. . . . We act as though the day were not happening. Neither of us will look at a clock. . . . I stand at the window all through the day, and Henk, on purpose, sits with his back to the window. When we sense that it's about five o'clock . . . we experience a sense of relief that the day is finished."

Anne Frank is today an icon of hope—a symbol known worldwide, and for good reason. Her spirit stands triumphant next to the harsh judgment history has rendered on the Nazis—and over all others who, even today, are guilty of crimes against humanity. Anti-Semitism continues to torment the Jews, and people the world over face persecution in its many guises. But if a young girl enduring a living hell could summon the power to imagine a future free of the horrors that surrounded her, then surely those who read her diary can summon the power to help make that day come to pass. As she wrote toward the end of her remarkable journal:

> It's really a wonder that I haven't dropped all my ideals, because they seem so absurd and impossible to carry out. Yet I keep them, because in spite of everything I still believe that people are really good at heart. I simply can't build up my hopes on a foundation consisting of confusion, misery, and death. I see the world gradually being turned into a wilderness, I hear the ever approaching thunder, which will destroy us too, I can feel the sufferings of millions and yet, if I look up into the heavens, I think that it will all come right, that this cruelty too will end, and that peace and tranquility will return again.

> In the meantime, I must uphold my ideals, for perhaps the time will come when I shall be able to carry them out.

Appendix I

Key to Diary Names and Real Names

To protect their privacy, Anne Frank gave false names to the real people she wrote about in her diary. Miep Gies, in her memoirs, *Anne Frank Remembered: The Story of the Woman Who Helped to Hide the Frank Family*, used the same false names that Anne had used. For the sake of clarity and consistency, the false names have been used throughout this text as well. Some historical documents and magazine and newspaper articles have used the real names. The following list is a key to the real-life names of the people appearing in Anne's diary.

Name given by Anne:	*Real name*:
Hermann Van Daan	Hermann van Pels
Petronella Van Daan	Petronella van Pels
Peter Van Daan	Peter van Pels
Albert Dussell	Friedrich Pfeffer
Miep van Santen	Hermine "Miep" Santrouschitz Gies
Henk van Santen	Jan Gies
Jo Koophuis	Johannes Kleiman
Victor Kraler	Victor Gustav Kugler
Elli Vossens	Bep Voskuijl
Lies Goosens	Hannah Elisabeth Pick-Goslar

Appendix II

The Diary's Popularity

Some of the languages and countries in which the diary has been published:

Arabic	Israel
Armenian	Soviet Union (now Commonwealth of Independent States)
Bengali	India
Catalan	Spain
Chinese	Taiwan
Czech	Czechoslovakia
Danish	Denmark, Greenland
Dutch	The Netherlands
English	Great Britain, United States
Esperanto	The Netherlands
Estonian	Soviet Union (now Commonwealth of Independent States)
Finnish	Finland
French	France
Georgian	Soviet Union (now Commonwealth of Independent States)
German	Germany, Switzerland
Greek	Greece
Hebrew	Israel
Hungarian	Hungary
Icelandic	Iceland
Italian	Italy
Japanese	Japan
Kazakh	Soviet Union (now Commonwealth of Independent States)
Korean	South Korea

Lithuanian	Soviet Union (now Commonwealth of Independent States)
Macedonian	Yugoslavia
Norwegian	Norway
Persian	Iran
Polish	Poland
Portuguese	Brazil, Portugal
Romanian	Romania
Russian	Soviet Union (now Commonwealth of Independent States)
Serbian	Yugoslavia
Slovenian	Czechoslovakia, Yugoslavia
Spanish	Argentina, Mexico, Spain, Uruguay
Swedish	Sweden
Thai	Thailand
Turkish	Turkey
Yiddish	Argentina, Israel, Poland, Romania

Source: Steenmeijer, Anneke, ed. *A Tribute to Anne Frank*. Garden City, NY: Doubleday, 1971.

Appendix III

Organizations

The Anne Frank Foundation sponsors programs and exhibitions concerning Anne Frank, the Holocaust, and other related subjects and is a clearinghouse for information. The American Friends of Anne Frank Center is the foundation's U.S. representative. They can be contacted in writing or by telephone at the following addresses:

ANNE FRANK FOUNDATION
Postbus 730,1000 AS
Amsterdam, The Netherlands
Phone: (20) 264533

AMERICAN FRIENDS OF ANNE FRANK CENTER
106 East 19th Street, 4th Floor
New York, NY 10003
Phone: (212) 529-9532

Further Reading

Dawidowicz, Lucy S. *The War Against the Jews 1933–1945*. New York: Free Press, 1986.

Frank, Anne. *The Diary of a Young Girl*. New York: Doubleday, 1967.

———. *Tales from the Secret Annex*. New York: Washington Square Press, 1983.

Gies, Miep, with Alison Leslie Gold. *Anne Frank Remembered: The Story of the Woman Who Helped to Hide the Frank Family*. New York: Simon & Schuster, 1987.

Lindwer, Willy. *The Last Seven Months of Anne Frank*. New York: Pantheon, 1991.

Maass, Walter B. *The Netherlands at War: 1940–1945*. New York: Abelard-Schuman, 1970.

The Netherlands State Institute for War Documentation. *The Diary of Anne Frank: The Critical Edition*. New York: Doubleday, 1989.

Presser, Jacob. *The Destruction of the Dutch Jews*. Translated by Arnold Pomerans. New York: Dutton, 1969.

Schloss, Eva, with Evelyn Julia Kent. *Eva's Story: A Survivor's Tale by the Step-Sister of Anne Frank*. New York: St. Martin's Press, 1988.

Schnabel, Ernst. *Anne Frank: A Portrait in Courage*. New York: Harcourt, Brace and World, 1958.

Steenmeijer, Anna G., ed. *A Tribute to Anne Frank*. Garden City, NY: Doubleday, 1971.

Chronology

1925	Otto Frank and Edith Holländer are married
February 16, 1926	Margot Betti Frank is born
June 12, 1929	Anneliese Marie Frank is born
March 1933	Adolf Hitler assumes full dictatorial powers in Germany
Summer 1933	The Franks leave Frankfurt for Aachen to stay with Edith's mother; Otto goes to Amsterdam to make arrangements for the family to settle there
December 1933	Edith and Margot join Otto at the family apartment on the Merwedeplein in Amsterdam
March 1934	Anne joins the family at the Merwedeplein
Nov. 9–10, 1938	Kristallnacht
September 1, 1939	Germany invades Poland, starting World War II
May 1940	The Netherlands is conquered and occupied by German troops
December 1941	The United States enters World War II after the Japanese attack on Pearl Harbor
April 29, 1942	Nazi decree is issued requiring all Dutch Jews to affix a yellow star reading *Jood* (Dutch for "Jew") to their clothing
June 12, 1942	Anne receives a diary as a gift for her 13th birthday
July 6, 1942	The Franks leave their apartment and go into hiding
February 2, 1943	The Germans surrender at the Battle of Stalingrad in the Soviet Union
June 6, 1944	D day, the Allied invasion of Normandy
August 4, 1944	The Franks are arrested and brought to the Westerbork transit camp
September 3, 1944	The Franks are shipped by train to the Auschwitz death camp in Poland
October 1944	Anne and Margot are transferred to Bergen-Belsen in Germany

January 6, 1945	Edith Frank dies at Auschwitz
Late February 1945	Margot Frank dies at Bergen-Belsen
Early March 1945	Anne Frank dies of typhus at Bergen-Belsen
May 7, 1945	The war in Europe ends with Germany's formal surrender
June 1945	Otto Frank, the only one of the eight in hiding to survive the war, arrives back in Amsterdam; after he hears of Anne's death, Miep Gies gives him the diaries she had found and stored away
August 1945	The war in the Pacific ends with Japan's surrender after atomic bombs obliterate Hiroshima and Nagasaki
June 1947	Anne's diaries are published in Amsterdam as *The Secret Annex*
1950	*The Secret Annex* is published in Germany and France
1952	The book is published in England and the United States under the title *Anne Frank: The Diary of a Young Girl*
1955	A play based on the diary is staged in New York and wins the Pulitzer Prize
August 19, 1980	Otto Frank dies in Switzerland at the age of 91
June 12, 1989	On the 60th anniversary of Anne's birthday, Doubleday publishes *The Diary of Anne Frank: The Critical Edition*

Index

PICTURE CREDITS

Richard Amdur is a writer with a continuing interest in Jewish affairs. For Chelsea House's WORLD LEADERS—PAST & PRESENT series he has written *Menachem Begin*, *Moshe Dayan*, and *Chaim Weizmann*. He has also written a biography of Golda Meir, published by Fawcett/Columbine. He is the author of *Wilderness Preservation* and *Toxic Materials* in Chelsea House's EARTH AT RISK series, and his articles have appeared in the *New York Times*, *Cosmopolitan*, and other periodicals. Amdur lives with his wife in Brooklyn, New York.

Vito Perrone is Director of Teacher Education and Chair of Teaching, Curriculum, and Learning Environments at Harvard University. He has previous experience as a public school teacher, a university professor of history, education, and peace studies (University of North Dakota), and as dean of the New School and the Center for Teaching and Learning (both at the University of North Dakota). Dr. Perrone has written extensively about such issues as educational equity, humanities curriculum, progressive education, and evaluation. His most recent books are: *A Letter to Teachers: Reflections on Schooling and the Art of Teaching*; *Enlarging Student Assessment in Schools*; *Working Papers: Reflections on Teachers, Schools, and Communities*; *Visions of Peace*; and *Johanna Knudsen Miller: A Pioneer Teacher*.

92
Fra

Amdur, Richard.

Anne Frank

25615

$18.95

DATE			